# Health Care Communication Using Personality Type

The importance of effective communication in health care, both with patients and with other professionals, has long been acknowledged. However, most models assume that the people with whom we communicate will react in the same way – what works for one person will be equally good for another.

In *Health Care Communication Using Personality Type*, **Judy Allen** and **Susan A. Brock** challenge this assumption. This ground-breaking book draws upon research data and examples from everyday health care situations to demonstrate that the behavior differences we all experience in others actually fit within a readily understandable framework (based on the Myers-Briggs Type Indicator®). Using this knowledge, health professionals can learn to vary the way in which they approach patients and colleagues, to break bad news more effectively and to encourage clients to follow clinical advice.

**Judy Allen MA RGN** is a researcher and consultant working with the Myers-Briggs Type Indicator in health care, with a special interest in oncology and palliative care. **Susan A. Brock Ph.D.** is an organizational consultant and licensed psychologist. She has researched, designed and written programs based on the Myers-Briggs Type Indicator, entitled FLEX Selling®, FLEX Talk® and FLEX Care®.

# Health Care Communication Using Personality Type
## Patients are different!

**Judy Allen and Susan A. Brock**

London and Philadelphia

First published 2000
by Routledge
11 New Fetter Lane, London EC4P 4EE

Simultaneously published in the USA and Canada
by Taylor & Francis Inc.
325 Chestnut Street, 8th Floor, Philadelphia, PA 19106

*Routledge is an imprint of the Taylor & Francis Group*

Typeset in Times New Roman by
Florence Production, Stoodleigh, Devon
Printed and bound in Great Britain by
TJ International Ltd, Padstow, Cornwall

*British Library Cataloguing in Publication Data*
A catalogue record for this book is available
from the British Library

*Library of Congress Cataloging in Publication Data*
Allen, Judy, 1947–
     Health Care communication using personality type: patients are different!/
Judy Allen and Susan A. Brock.
          p. cm.
     Includes bibliographical references and index.
     ISBN 0–415–21373–8 (hb)—ISBN 0–415–21374–6 (pbk.)
     1. Medical personnel and patient. 2. Patients—Psychology. 3. Myers-Briggs
Type Indicator. I. Brock, Susan A., 1947– II. Title.

R727.3.A44 2000
610.69'6—dc21                                                             99–055354

ISBN 0–415–21373–8 (hbk)
ISBN 0–415–21374–6 (pbk)

# Contents

# Illustrations

## Tables

## Figures

# Preface

We see this work as an opportunity to break new ground. In *Health Care Communication Using Personality Type* we combine a well-researched and respected framework for understanding normal differences in people with the practical need for interacting success-fully with patients and others in a health care setting.

Our backgrounds and interests dovetail in this practical collaboration. Brock's background is as an organizational psychologist, bringing applied psychology and its tools to management and organizational development. Her work over the past twenty-five years has focused on taking the knowledge of psychology and applying it to how people can successfully lead businesses, interact in teams, structure their organizations and teach others. She has worked in corporate settings and in higher education, including medical education, and has consulted internationally over the past fifteen years. Introduced to type preference and the Myers-Briggs Type Indicator® in 1979, she developed applications of the framework to practical influencing and sales. It was the training materials of FLEX Talk® and FLEX Selling® and the booklet *Using Type in Selling* that drew Allen to propose the current work.

Allen's background of thirty years in public and private health care gives her a well-rounded view of what practitioners face. In addition to early years as a practitioner working in both hospitals and the community, she has served as a nurse educator on a regional and national level. During that time, she has developed a particular interest in working with those professionals who provide specialist services in the fields of oncology and palliative care. She has also worked extensively in medically-based research. As a Myers-Briggs practitioner she has worked extensively in the area of communication training and has published a number of relevant papers reflecting this experience. Against this background, Allen recognized that a major contribution could be made by applying the framework of type preference, and Brock's prior work in particular, to health care communication. In addition to this book this recognition led to the development of FLEX Care®. Over the last ten years, models of patient listening and communication have proliferated. They have raised consciousness about the importance and difficulty of communicating not only with patients but also within the health care team. However, these models appear to assume that all recipients are "the same" – what will work for one person will work for another. As practitioners, we know that this is not the case. Successful practitioners naturally vary their approach.

As health care continues to increase in complexity, patients gain in sophistication and effective cross-discipline interaction becomes even more demanding, a straightforward, reliable framework for understanding differences with patients, families and co-workers is indispensable. This book is written to answer that need.

# Acknowledgements

We would like to extend our thanks to:

The individuals who filled out the questionnaires and those who were interviewed or involved in pilot FLEX Care® workshops.

We would also like to extend a special acknowledgement to Angela Nelson for her assistance in translating from one computer system to another, her complementary type perspective, and her support throughout the preparation of the manuscript.

# 1 Communication, health care and the perspective of type
## Introducing the theory

## Introduction

Consider the following four statements:

*   People prefer to communicate in different ways.
*   Most people have a preferred style of communication.
*   It is easier to communicate with some people than it is with others.
*   A system exists which provides a simple framework for understanding these differences.

Most of us would probably accept the first three statements with relative ease; the fourth may give more cause for thought.

It is clear that people prefer to communicate differently, as these two simple examples demonstrate:

*   Some people seem to have a great deal to say spontaneously on almost any subject, while others are deep in silent contemplation before responding.
*   Some people seem to speak from the heart, reflecting their values, while others are more reserved and factual in their communication.

When we spend time with others we come to recognize and even anticipate their possible reactions and may make this kind of comment to a third party:

> Well, I am really excited by our new ideas but I expect that when I present them at the meeting my boss will want to examine all the details contained in our proposal. You know she never likes the idea of major change and will go over everything line by line.

This takes us to the third statement: it is easier to communicate with some people than with others. The two people involved in the previous example appear to enjoy planning and talking about change in a conceptual way, while their "boss" appears more interested in the detail. They have interpreted this difference in a particular way – "she never likes the idea of change" – and are preparing themselves for a difficult session.

The fourth statement, the one that is more likely to raise doubt in our minds, may contain the key to this dilemma, although initially it may appear overly optimistic:

> A system which makes differences in communication style understandable, and it's *simple*?

Is there a system available, which explains why people might respond differently in the situations outlined above? If there were, would it assist nurses and allied health professionals in communication with patients?

The answer to both questions is a resounding "yes!"

In the past, there was an assumption that people entering the health care profession knew how to communicate with patients. Communication skills did not appear on the average curriculum. Nurse training, and that of other practitioners, was based on the acquisition of theoretical knowledge and practical skills and, in fact, those who talked to patients were often labeled lazy. Nurses in particular tended to be told what to do and they in turn told their patients what to do. Everyone involved was remarkably obedient!

Much has changed in the last decades; communication skills have become an integral part of training. At the same time, the clientele has become more critical and demanding and less inclined to be obedient or "spoken down" to. In response to these changes, health care providers have needed to change their approach to patients.

As the title *Healthcare Communication Using Personality Type* suggests, this book is intended to introduce and put to practical use the theory and practice of psychological type. In order to do this we will be introducing an instrument known as the Myers-Briggs Type Indicator® (MBTI®). This model of psychological type preference, first explored by Swiss psychologist Carl Jung, is used internationally to improve individual and team performance throughout industry, education, counseling and many other disciplines.

In this chapter, you will be introduced to this framework for understanding differences in people and how these differences affect behavior and communication. You will briefly explore the background of this framework. Examples from patient research will amplify the framework. Finally, using the framework, you will be able to begin to understand your own preferences and how they may have shaped your own reactions both as a professional and as a patient in health care situations.

When collecting data for this book we set out to discover how patients want to receive information and communicate with their caregiver. We asked neutral questions about how patients preferred to engage with their health care professional. For example, we asked:

> "How do you prefer to be communicated with in a health care setting?"

Although there was no invitation to censure, and indeed criticism was not the intended outcome of the study, there was a great deal of adverse comment. The following statement reflects a view shared by many:

> My experience is thankfully limited but I rarely feel as if I am being spoken to as an intelligent, professional person. I have found I had to assert myself and complain constructively (at times) and when using that strategy a different attitude then emanates. A lack of effective communication is evident in many health professionals, which I think adds to their stress, as they struggle to find ways of dealing with people.

There are a number of interesting points here. This respondent feels that he has to assert himself in order to receive the respect he requires. He recognizes that, when communication skills are lacking, stress increases not only for the patient but also for the staff. As the extract demonstrates, he is highly articulate and able to express his dissatisfaction in a way that few patients would.

One other respondent, having stated that she wanted as many details as possible about her treatment, ended:

> Of course, it is difficult, and not everyone would want the detail that I want. But that's what it means to be a professional and paid for being so; you've got to make judgments not just operate on autopilot.

These extracts highlight one of the main themes of the data:

> Treat me as an intelligent individual.

It is true that we tend to notice communication only when it stands out. That is, we notice it when the communication we receive is truly poor or quite outstanding. We make a note of it to others and ourselves. It may also be true that when we are in distress, such as in medical need, we are more aware of the communication that comes our way. Our FLEX Care® data points to this sensitivity. Patients notice the communication that comes their way and it can affect how they react to, and work with, their health care professional.

The importance of positive communication was also illustrated in one reply which indicated that a level of positive connection achieved by effective conversations provided healing:

> I have already said but want to say again that being fully listened to and heard is so important it feels as if it's part of the caring and healing process. Treat me as intelligent and as if feelings, facts and treatment ALL matter.

It is important to remember that not all patients want the same kind of communication. The information gathered from respondents in the US and UK demonstrates that people have varying needs and priorities when consulting with a health professional. What may be right for one patient may not be for another. Examples of this will be seen throughout the book.

This brings us back to the issue of looking for a system that provides a simple framework for understanding these differences. The Myers-Briggs Type Indicator (MBTI) can improve understanding and communication in very practical ways. It may help to summarize the task as follows:

- People are different.
- If we can understand these differences we can increase our effectiveness.
- The Myers-Briggs Type Indicator can be used as the framework with which to understand preferences and adapt responses to complement patient differences.

## Headline messages

- It is important to recognize, understand and value different styles of communication.

- If we can understand and value different approaches we may unlock qualities in both ourselves and the other person which will allow us to work more effectively and creatively together.
- Within the health care setting communication is fundamental to good care and good teamwork.

## A short history of the MBTI

### *Isabel Myers and Katharine Briggs*

The Myers-Briggs Type Indicator has been developed over a fifty-year period. The work began in the early part of this century as Isabel Myers and her mother, Katharine Briggs, brought their interest in individual differences together with careful study of Carl Jung's ideas on "psychological types."

Jung wrote:

> In my medical work . . . I have long been struck by the fact that besides the many individual difference in human psychology there are also typical differences.
>
> (Jung 1971)

He went on to develop this insight into a book, *Psychological Types*. While some of the language and depth of theory in this work may be experienced as daunting, certain phrases have a clarity and simplicity. For example, if we refer back to the two colleagues who enjoy the conceptual approach to change and cannot understand the different approach of their boss, Jung (1971) provides this insight:

> we naturally tend to understand everything in terms of our own type.

One of the original aims of Isabel Myers was to make the work of Jung accessible to a greater audience. Interestingly, many people now take the journey in the opposite direction, finding that an interest in personality type can lead to wanting to learn more about Jungian theory.

The major work on developing the MBTI commenced at the outbreak of the Second World War when:

Isabel Myers sought a way to help by finding a means for people to understand rather than destroy each other.

*(MBTI News* 1985)

On a practical level history records:

she saw many people taking jobs out of patriotism, but hating tasks which went against the grain instead of using their gifts.

*(MBTI News* 1985)

What Isabel Myers actually did was to devise a set of seemingly simple questions and test them on a small criterion group. She then reworked items, moving on to larger and more diverse groups, refining the instrument as part of a constant progression.

The development of the Indicator took twenty years of work, much of it carried out alone as she discovered patterns and meanings in the data. It is hard for us to imagine, living in a technologically assisted world, the feat of creating a complex psychological instrument using only an adding machine.

Health care workers were involved at an early stage and serve to illustrate the vast nature of the task, in that she collected type preference information from 10,000 nurses, again without a computer in sight! She also worked with medical students. Within a year of being invited into a number of medical schools, she "had given the Indicator to a total of 3,605 students" (Saunders 1991). These students became part of the extensive follow-up reliability and validity studies of the instrument, and over the years the medical samples continued to grow as new students joined and existing recruits were followed-up.

In one twelve-year study, she was able to determine:

Among other things, that most of the (medical) students had selected careers and kinds of practice that was attractive to their type.

(Saunders 1991)

Isabel Myers recognized the importance of those in the caring professions since she believed that:

accurate perception and informed judgment i.e. good type development [were] especially important in professionals who have others' lives in their hands.

*(MBTI News* 1985)

Despite the volume of work undertaken and the demonstrable insights achieved as her work progressed, she faced an uphill struggle. American psychology was in love with behaviorism and gave short shrift to European theories of personality. Jung's work was certainly not in the behaviorist camp. His work included such unmeasurable concepts as the "collective unconscious." In addition, Myers was not a psychologist, not an academic and not a male – three large barriers in the 1940s and 1950s. However, fueled by vision and sound research, Myers was able to gain the support of the Education Testing Service, an American organization of renown in psychological testing circles. With this support and dogged follow-through, Myers witnessed her work published during the 1960s and saw it become more widely appreciated in the following decade.

At the time of her death in 1980, she had completed her book, *Gifts Differing* – still considered a classic in MBTI terms – and continued to see the Indicator refined and researched. Her dream remained that people would come to understand that there is truly a "mutual usefulness of opposites" and that this would enhance individual understanding across all settings.

## Headline message

The framework of type preference is a way to understand normal differences. The Indicator is a tool for assessing those individual differences and has given millions of people a positive understanding of their own patterns of communication as well as an understanding of the mutual usefulness of differences.

## The Myers-Briggs Type Indicator (MBTI)

Having described the background surrounding the instrument and the intentions of its main author, we will now examine the instrument itself.

Those working with the MBTI often find themselves in difficulty when they tell others "it's not a test." When introduced to the MBTI, people find that it looks extraordinarily like a test in that there is a question booklet and an answer sheet. Furthermore, the questions are marked and counted or even computer scored. Although an elegant psychometric instrument or test, it is not a "test" from the standpoint of determining right or wrong answers or better or worse communication preferences.

The best way to describe the MBTI is as an instrument, which measures psychological preferences on four different scales:

- How one prefers to be energized
- What one prefers to pay attention to
- On what one initially bases a decision
- How one prefers to manage one's life

These scales are based on Jung's work, the last scale inferred by Myers from his body of writing. In order to define what is meant by "preference" in this context you might like to try an exercise for which you need a pencil and a scrap of paper.

- First, simply sign your name.
- Having done that, place the pencil in your other hand and sign again.

Think for a moment what differences you felt and noticed when you used your less preferred hand.

In workshops, this exercise usually leads to much laughter interspersed with a few groans. The responses include such words as "it feels:"

- Awkward/clumsy
- Childlike
- Smaller/larger than my usual signature
- Funny/playful

It is also often said that it takes longer and we have observed people taking time to angle the paper to make it easier.

One important comment, which comes up occasionally, is "it looks better."

In the context of the MBTI this exercise demonstrates that although the majority of us have a clear preference as to whether we use our left or right hand we *are* able to use the other one and, indeed, if we really try the results can be very good.

This leads to the notion of practice and development. If we diligently exercised our less preferred hand, it would improve greatly but, if we were asked unexpectedly to sign a document, for example, the chances are we would reach for our pen with our traditionally preferred hand. This parallels Jung's theory of opposites in aspects of personality. We use both poles but prefer one.

The most important things to remember about the MBTI are these:

- It is intended only to indicate preferences.
- It is designed to help people to be aware of their "gifts."
- It can assist in understanding and valuing those with different gifts.
- It provides a unique framework for individual development.
- It does not measure *amount* of a preference or *ability*, simply the preference itself.
- There are no good or bad preferences.

It is important to hold these points in mind as we move on to look at the specifics of the MBTI. Without this understanding, the instrument can appear to be limiting or judgmental. It is clear from what we know about Isabel Myers and Jungian type theory that a judgmental stance is in total opposition to these authors' thinking.

## The four scales

The questions in the MBTI booklet are measuring four different scales, namely:

| | | | |
|---|---|---|---|
| Extraversion | (E) | Introversion | (I) |
| Sensing | (S) | Intuition | (N) |
| Thinking | (T) | Feeling | (F) |
| Judging | (J) | Perceiving | (P) |

Each preference is identified in a shorthand form by its first letter. The exception is Intuition, which, because "I" is already used to represent Introversion, takes its second letter, "N."

As each scale is introduced, you might like to consider what you feel your own preference might be and you might find yourself thinking about the preferences of others whom you know well.

## Extraversion and Introversion – preferred source of energy

It is important to be precise about these particular words because they are in common usage and may mean different things to different people. At first sight, we may think Extraversion and Introversion refer to sociability. It is fairly common to consider Extraverts as people who are out and about, joining every club in sight, while their introverted counterparts are at home reading. Although this may in some sense be true, the full definition goes much deeper. Sociability may be seen as an effect rather than a cause. From the MBTI perspective, we are considering the preferred sources of energy, how we are more likely to gain our energy. Those with a preference for Extraversion tend to relate more to the outer world, gaining energy from being with people or things in the environment. Those with a preference for Introversion tend to focus on the inner world of ideas and need periods of solitude in order to recharge.

Pearman and Albritton (1997) have worked extensively with the MBTI and provide clearly-drawn examples of the differences:

> Extraverts are stimulus hungry. Extraverted minds seek external activity, change and interaction to create the energy needed to guide the self through the day.

The individual who prefers Introversion is aware of the internal world of experiences and is generally less in tune with the Extraverted energy field. Not only is the individual who has preferences for Introversion more aware of the inner world, but in fact they gain their energy and replenishment from it.

Recalling the name-signing exercise, it is important to emphasize that we all have, and need, access to both preferences. We may do so without even realizing our choices.

Brock has used common everyday words and phrases to explain type in her "Four-Part Framework" (Brock 1991). She uses the phrase "Talk it Out" to connote the preference for Extraversion. She uses the phrase "Think it Through" to connote a preference for Introversion.

*Table 1.1*    The Four-Part Framework®*

| Talk it Out (Extraversion) | Think it Through (Introversion) |
|---|---|
| **Specifics** (Sensing) | **Big Picture** (Intuition) |
| **Logical Implications** (Thinking) | **Impact on People** (Feeling) |
| **Joy of Closure** (Judging) | **Joy of Processing** (Perceiving) |

*Adapted from The Four-Part Framework®, by Susan A. Brock, Center for Applications of Psychological Type, 1987. Reprinted with permission.

Differences in communication, which as already discussed is of over-riding importance in health care settings, can be an expression of type. Extraverts have a tendency to "think out loud." An idea becomes fully formed when articulated. Often, an idea which is at a provisional stage may be heard by others as being final – a situation which can cause confusion. A nurse with an extraverted preference once remarked:

> As I hear these ideas coming out of my mouth, I am thinking ... half of this is wrong.

Patients with a preference for Introversion, on the other hand, may reflect on ideas in what Pearman and Albritton describe as an internal "Japanese garden" where the ideas can be pondered and refined. By the time information is shared, therefore, a lot of thought may have gone into it. This, however, can also have its problems since the ideas may never be shared. It might even be the case that a patient with a preference for Introversion has thought about something for so long that they believe it has been shared when it has not.

In summary, we might see ourselves or those patients with a preference for Extraversion as being:

- Easy to engage in conversation
- Easy to know, at least to some level
- Not always able to listen, tending to interrupt
- Preferring more rather than less verbal communication and feedback

Those with an Introverted preference, on the other hand, may be seen as being:

- Less easy to engage in conversation
- Harder to know, conversations may include long pauses
- Less overtly in need of communication
- Liking written information

Or, as Pearman and Albritton (1997) put it:

> The kernel of truth is that Extraversion seeks to initiate and Introversion is inclined to receive and reflect.

*Your preference*

You may want to hypothesize your preference on this dimension of how you energize. Remembering you do both, the following behavior cues may help you understand your "first stop" or preference.

## Extraversion and Introversion – behavior cues

☐ **Talk it out**            ☐ **Think it through**

Rapid speech                 Pauses while giving information

Appears to "think aloud"     Quieter voice volume

Interrupts                   Shorter sentences – not run on

Louder volume of voice

(FLEX Talk® 1991 Revised 1999, Brock Associates,<br>Minneapolis, Minnesota, 55436, USA)

You may also see yourself as more like one of the individuals in the examples below.

### Talk it Out (Extraversion)

• At meetings, I know I talk too much, and often cannot stop myself. I also sometimes hear myself saying something which I was not even aware of thinking.
• When I go to meetings, I often feel I have to say something to fill the gap in conversation. I often wonder what the quiet people are thinking and why they don't contribute.
• I enjoy meetings; it is a chance to talk things over. I learn a lot from doing that.

### Think it Through (Introversion)

• I find myself preparing for hours before meetings, it is the only way I can keep up with the conversation.
• I sometimes want to say something during the meeting but by the time I am ready to speak, they are talking about something else.
• I am often surprised to hear people talking about things they haven't really considered fully. I just can't do that.

These differences in the ways people are energized can lead to very different styles of communication, and an understanding of the varying approaches can improve mutual understanding. Before moving on, you might like to reflect on this section, your own preference and the ways in which you have observed Extraversion and Introversion being played out.

## Sensing and Intuition – what one pays attention to

Sensing and Intuition are referred to in type theory as the perceiving functions. They describe the different ways in which people gather information and direct their attention.

Sensing, as the name implies, relies on the five senses. Those with this preference attend to facts and details. In Brock's Four-Part Framework, the key word is "Specifics." Sensing types tend to be focused in the present and to concentrate on practical tasks. The general sense is a practical "if it is not broken, don't fix it" attitude. Pearman and Albritton (1997) describe those with this preference as being "drawn to facts like metal to magnets; they feel an urge for clarity."

Those with a Sensing preference may ask for detailed, factual information about the current situation and not care for speculation or conjecture. They may exhibit interest in the practical matters of today rather than the future possibilities which they may find irrelevant or stressful. Sensing types tend to value that which is tried and tested rather than things experimental. Their questions focus on clarifying "what is, how many, what has been done already?" For example, a patient with a preference for Sensing may want to see their results, know exactly what a normal result would be. Should they require treatment, they may want to ask how successful the proposed regime has been in other cases.

Intuition, in contrast, tends to focus on possibilities and what "might be" rather than detail and "what is." As Brock's Four-Part Framework would suggest, those with this preference are inclined to identify with the "Big Picture." Intuitives like to identify patterns and tend to enjoy variety, possibilities and that which is unique. What has been done before may be perceived as dull.

Those with a preference for Intuition are more likely to start with conceptual questions about the overall situation and may become visibly irritated or fatigued with detail. They may be observed to "switch off" if over-loaded with data.

The intuitive perception trusts ideas like the eyes trust light. The striving for the association of ideas is often so strong that, like two sticks rubbing together to create fire, Intuition creates innovation.

(Pearman and Albritton 1997)

In summary, we might see those patients with a preference for Sensing as:

• Interested in factual details of their condition
• Preferring step-by-step explanation
• Asking practical questions

Those with a preference for Intuition are more likely to:

• Ask long-term, speculative questions
• Seek new solutions (for example, alternative or complementary medicine)
• Want multiple options

### *Your preference*

You may want to hypothesize your preference on this dimension of what you prefer to pay attention to. Remembering you do both, the following behavior cues may help you understand your "first stop" or preference.

## Sensing and Intuition – behavior cues

| ☐ **Specifics** | ☐ **Big Picture** |
|---|---|
| Asks for step-by-step information or instruction | Asks for current and long-range implications |
| Asks "what," "how" questions | Asks "why" questions |
| Uses precise descriptions | Talks in general terms |

(FLEX Talk 1991 Revised 1999, Brock Associates, Minneapolis, Minnesota, 55436, USA)

You may see yourself as more like one of the individuals in the following example which describes two different experiences of the same situation. The differences in perception are described differently by those with a preference for Sensing versus Intuition, as shown below:

*Specifics (Sensing)*

- When I am interviewing, I think it is important to have a list of questions to ask each candidate. I believe we should ask them about their background and whether they have done this kind of work before. It is important to hear examples of what they have actually done. I think the same questions should be put to each one in turn and that each interviewer should know which ones to ask. In this way, we get a clear picture of each candidate.

*Big Picture (Intuition)*

- I believe we should have an overall plan for an interview so that we can get as full a picture of each candidate as we can. To do this we need to ask general questions, why they applied for the position, what they can contribute. It is important to know in what way each candidate might contribute to the future of our organization. We should give hypothetical situations so we can get a feel for what the candidate thinks is important. I find a prepared list of questions and a detailed plan of the interview very restricting.

## Thinking and Feeling – a basis for decision making

Thinking and Feeling are described in Jungian terms as the judging functions because they represent two different ways of weighing decisions. Bayne (1995 ) correctly describes the Thinking and Feeling scale as being:

> most open to misinterpretation, as "not having emotions" and "not able to be logical," respectively.

This potential for misunderstanding and bias may provide a particularly important consideration for those working in health care, since coming to a conclusion and taking action are often the goal of a health intervention. It is for this reason that more detail will be given about this scale.

Those with a preference for Thinking tend to base their decisions on logical cause and effect thinking, described by Brock (1994) as "if this . . . then that." The Four-Part Framework phrase for a Thinking preference is "Logical Implications." Those with a preference for Thinking tend to analyze their situation in a non-personal manner. When communicating they are likely to be detached and task-centered and may well appear critical when examining an idea. The word "Thinking" in MBTI terms is referred to as "T" and it is often said that "T is for testing you!" Justice is a value much prized by Thinking types, as is competence.

Faced with illness, either their own or that of a loved one, those with a Thinking preference may be seen as objective, seeking logical, truthful explanations. This may be misinterpreted, particularly in relatives, as uncaring. Those with this preference describe themselves as being outside a situation looking in, needing to analyze events and make sense of what is happening. Under pressure, they may become increasingly critical of everyone and everything, particularly if there is a hint of incompetence. Additionally, any perceived injustice in the situation may be a particular problem for this type. For example, an individual with a Thinking preference might say "Why did I get this condition at this time, just as I was starting college?" While anyone is likely to experience this kind of feeling, it is particularly acute for this type.

One other facet of the Thinking function identified by Brock is "T" humor. This humor is often sharp, dark, even competitive: "who can be the cleverest and funniest?" One patient, dying from a rapid ovarian cancer, said to her grieving husband:

> You know this is a terrible illness, I can't drink, I can't eat and I can't even have sex.

A British journalist, John Diamond, also provides illustrations of this humor. He had been suffering from cancer and describes a day when he became aware that his condition had deteriorated. On arriving for his appointment he was shown into a particularly well-furnished consulting room:

> . . . we knew it was all up . . . you do not ask for your patients to be taken to the comfy chairs if you're about to tell them that after all the shadow on their lung was a packet of Woodbines left on the machine by one of the cleaners.
>
> (Diamond 1999)

He continued by relating the fact that a physician accompanied his surgeon:

> I've known for a long time that if a medical doctor turned up . . . we were no longer talking about cure but remission.

Accompanying my surgeon were two men I'd not met before, a consultant oncologist and his registrar. Standing behind them, looking embarrassed was a tallish man in hood and gown with a scythe over his shoulder.

When given the news, which was indeed bad, he continues:

I could ask for a second opinion, I suppose, but quite honestly, it's bad enough having one expert telling you you're going to die without bringing in a second to rub it in.

Referring back to Bayne's comment about the potential for misunderstanding, this type of dark humor can be mistaken for a lack of finer feelings. In fact it may well be a safety valve.

The potential strength of this preference was equally well illustrated by the woman from the first example who was being cared for at home. In the middle of the night, perched precariously on the toilet seat, she gave her husband a wry smile and said:

Well, I don't think we can manage this any longer. Tomorrow I'll go to the hospice.

And she did.

John Diamond also displays this strength by writing openly about his condition and describing fears that anyone might have in such a way as to make them more acceptable.

Those with a preference for Feeling tend to base their decisions on "values that center on people" (Brock 1994). Conclusions tend to be sought through a subjective process, identifying what will please others or what is the person-centered value. Recognizing another's personal needs and expressing appreciation are of great importance for those with this preference. MBTI workshop participants illustrate this routinely by answering the question "what do you like to be praised for?" with answers which include "myself . . . how I've made a difference for others . . . for being myself." Harmony is important to Feeling types. This was demonstrated in a teaching setting recently where a role-play of an acrimonious telephone conversation was taking place. An observer with a clear preference for Feeling said that, although she was not directly involved, she had almost left the room because she felt so uncomfortable.

Patients with this preference are likely to wish to please their caregivers and are likely in their turn to appreciate praise. They may, however, have great difficulty in discussing, accepting or imparting "bad news." They may well base this on an idea that someone else may be upset whereas in fact the difficulty may be their own. Using an analogy from a different setting, a Feeling type described a course evaluation form as a "happy sheet." Similar metaphors may be adopted to describe illnesses or symptoms, avoiding the actual names of conditions. For example, one mother with a preference for Feeling explained:

> Although I knew my son's brain was not fully developed it took me two years to use the word "handicap." Once I got used to that, they changed it to "learning disability" and then "learning difficulty." I liked those even less.

Good relationships with carers may be so important for Feeling types that, for example, they will not complain directly when they perceive things to be wrong. This is particularly apparent when a long-term professional relationship is at stake, or one involving regular personal contact where harmony seems so important. An individual with a Feeling preference is more likely to discuss the problem with a third party who then deals with the problem. This, unwittingly, can cause the exact situation that the patient sought to avoid.

A woman, with a preference for Feeling, was discussing her fatal illness with a nurse. First, she said:

> I bought my husband, Steve, a gold watch for Christmas, because I won't be here next Christmas.

A few moments later, she added:

> I am not going to stay with my sister in Hong Kong this year; I would rather go next year.

When the nurse gently reflected back the two statements, she said:

> They are all so important to me; I try not to think about it if I can. It just makes everyone unhappy.

This woman demonstrated clearly the importance of Feeling or person-oriented values. They took precedence over logic.

Pearman and Albritton (1997) sum up an important feature in the contrasting worlds of those with a preference for Thinking and those who prefer Feeling:

For the Feeling type, competency is basically assumed and regular expressions of appreciation are needed; for the Thinking type, appreciation is basically assumed and need only be confirmed by . . . increases in responsibility.

In summary, patients with a preference for Thinking may be seen as:

- Asking logical questions
- Initially business-like rather than friendly
- "Testing" your competency

while those with a preference for Feeling are more likely to:

- Appear warm and friendly
- Seek a relationship with you
- Want to please

We began this chapter by emphasizing the importance of recognizing that people who have a Thinking preference are able to be sensitive and caring and that those with a preference for Feeling are able to be logical. This understanding is of crucial importance. It is equally valuable to recognize that both functions have equal value. One of our respondents, with a Feeling preference, explained:

Thinking–Feeling is the touchiest pair, I think because our society tends to value logic over everything and emotion recognition is seen as a weakness.

In addition, there is a strong gender bias associated with this dimension which does not attach to the other three. It is often felt that men should have a Thinking preference, while women should have a Feeling preference. Overall, studies show that, in fact, more males do verify a preference for Thinking and more females verify a preference for Feeling. This is the one dimension that shows a gender difference. Often MBTI practitioners have difficulty in providing feedback on this scale in that both men and women experience problems in "owning" Feeling and Thinking preferences respectively.

### Your preference

You may want to hypothesize your preference on this dimension of how you prefer to reach decisions. Remembering you do both, the following behavior cues may help you understand your "first stop" or preference.

## Thinking and Feeling – behavior cues

☐ **Logical Implications**

Appears to be "testing you" or your knowledge

Weighs the objective evidence

Not impressed that others have decided in favor

Conversations follow a pattern of logic – "if this, then that"

☐ **Impact on People**

Strives for harmony in interaction

May talk about what they value

Asks how others acted/resolved the situation

Matters to them whether others have been taken into account

(FLEX Talk 1991 Revised 1999, Brock Associates, Minneapolis, Minnesota, 55436, USA)

You may see yourself as more like one of the following individuals in this example which describes two different experiences of the same situation.

### *Logical Implications (Thinking)*

• When I visit the doctor, I want to know he really understands my case, is experienced and knowledgeable about it. I don't want him to humor me, just give me information about my problem and what can be done about it. I want to be treated as an intelligent adult and that means being told the truth.

### *Impact on People (Feeling)*

• I prefer it if the doctor knows about me and my case and shows an interest in me personally. I want to know about my condition and how other people have reacted to the proposed treatment. I prefer a kindly approach, sometimes I feel hurt by blunt comments.

## Judging and Perceiving – preferences for managing one's life

This final scale demonstrates different approaches to the way in which individuals manage their lives.

Those with a preference for Judging tend to live life in an organized, planned manner. They like to structure situations. They are
usually more comfortable after decisions have been made than they
are during the process. Brock's Four-Part Framework describes those
with this preference as having "A Joy of Closure" and as using words
that end in "ed," such as planned, arranged, organized. These words
suggest being "done." In everyday life Judging types are motivated
by goals which they prefer to achieve before any deadline.

In a health care situation those with a Judging preference may
want to move into action as fast as possible. They may be disturbed
by waiting for results of tests or indeed by waiting for treatment to
show effectiveness.

Faced with a life-threatening illness those with this preference are
likely to need to have "their affairs in order." Similarly, where the
immediate caregiver has this preference they may be particularly
insistent that the patient has indeed put their "affairs in order" and
may be frustrated if this is not accomplished. In general terms Judging
types are likely to prefer caregivers who are punctual and reliable
while they themselves may well be more reliable in terms of overall
compliance. An experienced palliative care nurse raised a more fundamental question in a type workshop:

> Is it likely that a person with a preference for Judging may be
> the one who wants to know fairly precisely how long they or
> their relative will live for, who will press for the information
> and be angry if it turns out to be inaccurate?

Others nodded assent and it appeared that this might provide one
tentative answer to a puzzle which had taxed many: should one give
specifics based on timelines based on known data? A doctor amplified this:

> I have learned how important it is not to give a time, even when
> patients ask me to. This is particularly important with some
> people; for example, I once said to a patient and his wife, "We
> are looking at weeks not months." They told me later that they
> read that as three weeks. When you think about it though we
> usually say six weeks, not a month and a half. I did not mean
> three weeks. It taught me to be honest but not exact.

In contrast, those with a preference for Perceiving are referred to
as the "go with the flow" people; one MBTI cartoon pictures a

Perceiving type in a boat gently moving down the stream. For those with this preference early decisions can be restrictive; they enjoy the actual process involved in decision making and can be led off on a new course by a new idea or situation. Perceiving types tend to prefer matters to be flexible and open while tending to become involved in too many different projects at once. All of this means that they often need to meet deadlines at the last minute. Brock describes the language of Perceiving types as "ing-ing" – wondering, planning, considering. The Four-Part Framework phrase for Perceiving is "Joy of Processing."

In a health care setting, those with a preference for Perceiving may want lots of information. They may well have more difficulty with adherence, finding treatment schedules restrictive, or they may ask to change their treatment schedules to fit other aspects of their life. Those with this preference are more likely to be able to deal with altered appointment times and are more tolerant of delay, indeed may even cause delay! Professional caregivers may observe that Perceiving types are less likely to focus immediately on their affairs – "there's plenty of time for that." Finally, it seems possible that the "how long have I got?" question, which may not in fact be asked, might require a more general response.

In summary, patients with a preference for Judging may be seen as:

• Needing definite answers
• Punctual
• Organized
• Making decisions well ahead of time

while those with a Perceiving preference are more likely to:

• Be flexible and open to new ideas and suggestions
• Arrive at the last minute, or after
• Put less emphasis on organization
• Make decisions only when it's time, as they see it

### *Your preference*

You may want to hypothesize your preference on this dimension of the way in which you manage your life. Remembering you do both, the following behavior cues may help you understand your "first stop" or preference.

## Judging and Perceiving – behavior cues

| ☐ Joy of Closure | ☐ Joy of Processing |
|---|---|
| Consistently early or on time for appointments | May be late for appointments or forget the time during an appointment |
| Impatient with overly long descriptions or procedures | Seems to want "space" to make own decisions |
| The tone is "let's get it done" | Feels put off by closing a conversation before they're ready |
| May even decide prematurely | Generally won't decide until the last moment |
| Uses "ed" words: "looked, compared, evaluated" | Uses "ing" words; "looking comparing, exploring" |

(FLEX Talk 1991 Revised 1999, Brock Associates, Minneapolis, Minnesota, 55436, USA)

You may see yourself as more like one of the following individuals in this example, which describes two different experiences of the same situation.

### *Joy of Closure (Judging)*

• When we held a meeting to discuss our plans for an open house at the hospital I wanted to simply decide the date and time, what exhibitions (which we had already identified at the last meeting) we would mount where. I had prepared a list of what I thought we should include and got very annoyed when other people started to waffle about new ideas and about extending the scope of the day.

### *Joy of Processing (Perceiving)*

• Driving to the meeting about our forthcoming open house, it occurred to me that we could develop our main theme, that of making the public more aware of what we do, in a better way. When I got there I explained my new ideas but was told we had already made a decision at the last meeting. I didn't see it like that at all, it seemed to me we should examine all the ideas we can before deciding what to do.

## Seeing the scales in combination

When the four scales are combined, sixteen "types" emerge. This is illustrated in Table 1.2. Two important points emerge at this stage. First, as we all know, there are more than sixteen types of people in the world. Type simply reflects one explanation for behaviors, which may otherwise appear random. There are, of course, many other sources for behavioral differences, such as upbringing, current health and many external features.

When these aspects of type preference are combined they lead to certain behaviors which can be reliably measured and observed. Table 1.3 contains short descriptions of behaviors related to each preference combination.

It is also important to understand that no one is confined to one type. The type table can be seen as a "sixteen-room house" in which each person has a "favorite room." We might say that we all go to all rooms, including the bathroom but we might not want to live there! The type framework is an excellent way of recognizing one's favorite room and of understanding the need to move into other rooms, or modes, as the occasion warrants.

Metaphorically this favorite room is "well-furnished," just as we would like it. When we can, we tend to go there. We also go to all

*Table 1.2*   The Myers-Briggs type table*

| | | | |
|------|------|------|------|
| ISTJ | ISFJ | INFJ | INTJ |
| ISTP | ISFP | INFP | INTP |
| ESTP | ESFP | ENFP | ENTP |
| ESTJ | ESFJ | ENFJ | ENTJ |

*Key*:
E = Extraversion   I  = Introversion
S = Sensing        N = Intuition
T = Thinking       F = Feeling
J  = Judging       P = Perceiving

of the other fifteen rooms. Our type simply reflects the room to which we naturally gravitate when we are free to do what we wish as we go about our daily activities and responsibilities. This perspective of using all the preferences is especially important in working with others. The aim is never to label or pigeonhole. Rather the aim is to understand the other person and gain perspective in order to interact more effectively.

Because observing, not labeling, is the key, it is not necessary to know another's type preference. It is only necessary to watch for behavior cues in the moment, remembering that the person may be visiting another room in their "house" and will want to be treated in accordance with their current room.

## Exercise

This short exercise is designed to help you to begin to apply type theory in a practical way.

1   Reflect for a few moments on your own experiences *as a patient*, preferably one good experience and one less good. It may help to make some notes. Taking the good experience first, consider the following:
    •   What struck you as particularly positive about this exchange?
    •   Can you identify any behavior cues exhibited by the practitioner?
    •   Do they match your own identified preferences?
    Turning to the less good experience:
    •   What was it that you found difficult about this exchange?
    •   Can you identify any behavior cues exhibited by the practitioner?
    •   Do they match your own preferences and, if not, how did that affect you? What would you have liked to have had done differently?
2   Consider now what your own preferences might be and how they might affect your communication with the patients with whom you are working.
3   Is there any connection between your needs as a patient and the way you tend to give information to your patients? An example, given to us by a newly-qualified doctor, may assist with this:

It's difficult for me to think as a patient ... I suppose that's because I speak to them in the way that I would want to be

*Table 1.3* Characteristics frequently associated with each type*

| ISTJ | ISFJ | INFJ | INTJ |
|---|---|---|---|
| Quiet, serious, earn success by thoroughness and dependability. Practical, matter-of-fact, realistic, and responsible. Decide logically what should be done and work toward it steadily regardless of distractions. Take pleasure in making everything orderly and organized - their work, their home, their life. Value traditions and loyalty. | Quiet, friendly, responsible, and conscientious. Committed and steady in meeting their obligations. Thorough, painstaking and accurate. Loyal, considerate, notice and remember specifics about people who are important to them, concerned with how others feel. Strive to create an orderly and harmonious environment at work and at home. | Seek meaning and connection in ideas, relationships and material possessions. Want to understand what motivates people and are insightful about others. Conscientious and committed to their firm values. Develop a clear vision about how best to serve the common good. Organized and decisive in implementing their vision. | Have original minds and great drive for implementing their ideas and achieving their goals. Quickly see patterns in external events and develop long-range explanatory perspectives. When committed, organize a job and carry it through. Skeptical and independent, determined, have high standards of competence and performance for themselves and others. |

| ISTP | ISFP | INFP | INTP |
|---|---|---|---|
| Tolerant and flexible, quiet observers until a problem appears and then act quickly to find workable solutions. Analyze what makes things work and readily get through large amounts of data to isolate the core of practical problems. Interested in cause and effect, organize facts using logical principles, value efficiency. | Quiet, friendly, sensitive and kind. Enjoy the present moment, what is going on around them. Like to have their own space and to work within their own time-frame. Loyal and committed to their values and to people who are important to them. Dislike disagreements and conflicts, do not force their opinions or values on others. | Idealistic, loyal to their values and to people who are important to them. Want an external life that can be congruent with their values. Curious, quick to see possibilities, can be catalysts for implementing ideas. Seek to understand people and to help them fulfill their potential. Adaptable, flexible and accepting unless a value is threatened. | Seek to develop logical explanations for everything that interests them. Theoretical and abstract, interested more in ideas than in social interaction. Quiet, contained, flexible and adaptable. Have unusual ability to focus in depth, to solve problems in their area of interest. Skeptical, sometimes critical, always analytical. |

## ESTP

Flexible and tolerant, they take a pragmatic approach focused on immediate results. Theories and conceptual explanations bore them – they want to act energetically to solve the problem. Focus on the here-and-now, spontaneous, enjoy each moment that they can be active with others. Enjoy material comforts and style. Learn best through doing.

## ESTJ

Practical, realistic, matter-of-fact. Decisive, quickly move to implement decisions. Organize projects and people to get things done, focus on getting results in the most efficient way possible. Take care of routine details. Have a clear set of logical standards, systematically follow them through and want others to also. Forceful in implementing their plans.

## ESFP

Outgoing, friendly and accepting. Exuberant lovers of life, people, and material comforts. Enjoy working with others to make things happen. Bring common sense and a realistic approach to their work and make work fun. Flexible and spontaneous, adapt readily to new people and environments. Learn best by trying a new skill with other people.

## ESFJ

Warm hearted, conscientious and cooperative. Want harmony in their environment, work with determination to establish it. Like to work with others to complete tasks accurately and on time. Loyal, follow through even in small matters. Notice what others need in their day-to-day lives and try to provide it. Want to be appreciated for who they are and for what they contribute.

## ENFP

Warmly enthusiastic, and imaginative. See life as full of possibilities. Make connections between events and information very quickly and confidently proceed based on the patterns they see. Want a lot of affirmation from others, and readily give appreciation and support. Spontaneous and flexible, often rely on their ability to improvise and their verbal fluency.

## ENFJ

Warm, empathetic, responsive and responsible. Highly attuned to the emotions, needs and motivations of others. Find potential in everyone, want to help others to fulfill their potential. May act as catalysts for individual and group growth. Loyal, responsive to praise and criticism. Sociable, facilitate others in a group and provide inspiring leadership.

## ENTP

Quick, ingenious, stimulating, alert, outspoken. Resourceful in solving new and challenging problems. Adept at generating conceptual possibilities and then analyzing them strategically. Good at reading other people. Bored by routine, will seldom do the same thing the same way, apt to turn to one new interest after another.

## ENTJ

Frank, decisive, assume leadership readily. Quickly see illogical and inefficient procedures and policies, develop and implement comprehensive systems to solve organizational problems. Enjoy long-term planning and goal setting. Usually well informed, well read, enjoy expanding their knowledge and passing it on to others. Forceful in presenting their ideas.

spoken to . . . oh, I see now, there's no real difference between what I do and what I would want for myself.

Does that mirror your experience?

(This is an issue that will be addressed in more detail in later chapters.)

4   Make a note of the insights that you have gained into the application of type so far and any outstanding questions you might have.

## Summary

In this chapter we have discussed:

* The importance of communication in health care
* The fact that personality type theory provides a framework useful to health care providers
* The background to the Myers-Briggs Type Indicator (MBTI)
* The structure of the MBTI

We have also provided you with an opportunity to consider what your own preferences might be and how they could affect your communication as both a patient and a practitioner. In the next chapter, we will turn to looking more directly at how to use the framework of type in health care communication.

Please note:
Myers-Briggs Type Indicator® and MBTI® are registered trademarks of Consulting Psychologists Press, Palo Alto, California, USA.

FLEX Selling®, FLEX Talk® and FLEX Care® are registered trademarks of Brock Associates, 5429 West Highwood Drive, Minneapolis, Minnesota MN 55436.

Introduction to Type® is a registered trademark of Consulting Psychologists Press Inc., Palo Alto.

---

# 2    Introducing FLEX Care

We have now spent some time learning about the Myers-Briggs Type Indicator in the context of health care communication. You may, by now, have some idea of your own type preferences. You may also have used this as an opportunity to reflect on your own needs as a patient or a member of a health care team.

It is likely, as was indicated in the notes provided with the exercise in the previous chapter, that you will have found that there is a link between your own preferences and the needs you might have as a patient. As practitioners we often communicate with patients in the way in which we ourselves prefer to receive communication. It might help to return to an example mentioned in the previous chapter, which described a newly-qualified doctor who found learning about personality type theory very helpful. When she reflected on her communication style, she commented:

> It's difficult for me to think as a patient ... I suppose that's because I speak to them in the way that I would want to be spoken to ... oh, I see now, there's no real difference between what I do and what I would want for myself.

This captures the link between our own preferences, how *we* like to receive communication, and how we are most likely to impart information to others. This, of course, works well provided we all share the same preferences but, needless to say, more often than not we don't.

To provide health professionals with a practical tool for enhanced communication, this chapter will detail type preference and how it maps onto a general communication framework. We will explore how different types vary in what they want in a health care situation. In addition, in order to use type and "flex" appropriately the practitioner must be able to spot type in action. Specific behavior cues to "type mode" will be reiterated and suggestions for interaction will be given.

## The basis for FLEX Care

The model which applies type preference to health care communication is called FLEX Care. Investigations into whether type preference affects communication were focused on general practical influencing situations: leading, working in teams, coaching, managing, sales, consulting and the like. Originally data were gathered from several hundred individuals who had verified their type preference. They were asked "How do you prefer to be sold to?" or "How do you prefer to be influenced in practical influencing situations?" These investigations stemmed from the observation that different types literally use different words to express similar meanings and as a result often have difficulty communicating with each other. The responses were analyzed as to whether any aspects of type helped to cluster the responses. These were early investigations into what now seems an obvious and reliable pattern recorded from several thousand individuals. Each aspect of type contributed to an aspect of communication and could be mapped onto a four-stage communication framework:

Stage 1        Initiating the interaction
Stages 2 & 3  Investigating needs and suggesting a course of action
Stage 4        Moving to commitment – next steps or closure

Data were then collected relating type to health care. Individuals were asked to answer questions including "What's most important to me?" in a variety of health care situations. (See the Appendix for the questionnaire.) The same pattern found in general influencing and communication situations was found in health care situations.

Figure 2.1 illustrates these four stages of creating commitment and shows which aspects of type are most relevant at each stage.

Each communication stage and its relationship to type will be briefly reviewed below. You may want to think about how your own type preferences usually show up and how you may have learned naturally to "flex" given the cues you pick up in the interaction. It is important to remember that we all use all the preferences. When we or our patients move from our natural preference to another, that is called type "mode." We can come to know our own type preference; however, with patients we simply note the mode they seem to be showing at any given time.

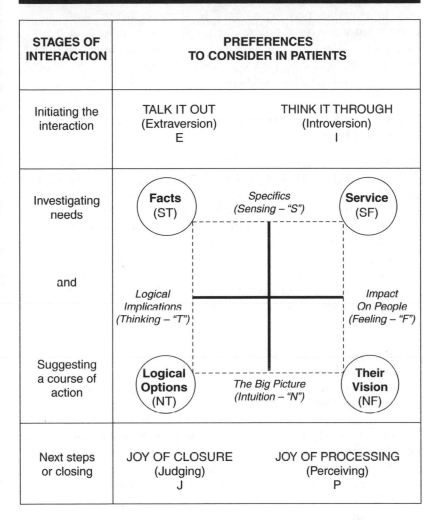

| STAGES OF INTERACTION | PREFERENCES TO CONSIDER IN PATIENTS | |
|---|---|---|
| Initiating the interaction | TALK IT OUT (Extraversion) E | THINK IT THROUGH (Introversion) I |
| Investigating needs | Facts (ST)    *Specifics (Sensing – "S")* | Service (SF) |
| and | *Logical Implications (Thinking – "T")* | *Impact On People (Feeling – "F")* |
| Suggesting a course of action | Logical Options (NT)    *The Big Picture (Intuition – "N")* | Their Vision (NF) |
| Next steps or closing | JOY OF CLOSURE (Judging) J | JOY OF PROCESSING (Perceiving) P |

*Figure 2.1* The Four-Part Framework © and Health Care Communication in FLEX Care ®, 2000, Brock Associates, Minneapolis, MN 55436, USA

## Stage 1: Initiating the interaction

The first stage, initiating the interaction, often includes an arrival, a short greeting, perhaps a handshake and then a settling in to the physical surroundings. It is in this initiation stage that Extraversion and Introversion play a major role. Extraverts, or those in an extraverted mode, prefer more energy to be shown, such as a faster verbal pace, more body animation and closer physical interaction, than do Introverts. Introverts may use fewer words, and be comfortable with more physical distance.

## Stages 2 and 3: Investigating needs and Suggesting a course of action

As the process moves forward into the stages of investigating needs and suggesting a course of action, people look for information to be presented in their preferred mode and for their process of coming to a conclusion or a decision to be honored. This is the heart of any communication or practical influencing process. The type aspects closely linked to the heart of communication are the four combinations of Perceiving and Judging preferences. In the Myers-Briggs framework these elements are called functions. Sensing (S) and Intuition (N) are the perceiving functions. Thinking (T) and Feeling (F) are the judging functions. The four combinations are called functional pairs:

Sensing and Thinking   (ST)
Sensing and Feeling    (SF)
Intuition and Feeling  (NF)
Intuition and Thinking (NT)

Because these appear to be the most important aspects of type for communication, the functional pairs will be discussed at greater length later in this chapter. Examples of how individuals with these preferences want to be worked with will also be given.

## Stage 4: Next steps or Closing

Finally, at the stage of moving to closure and setting out the next steps, there appears to be a link with the Judging and Perceiving preferences. Patients with a Judging preference, or in a judging mode, may want to move as rapidly as possible to closure. People with a

Perceiving preference, or in a perceiving mode, often have a variable pace linked to whether closure is actually seen as necessary or whether remaining open is more beneficial.

## Establishing purpose – the heart of the communication process

The heart of the communication process is establishing purpose. In the four-stage communication model just reviewed, establishing purpose is accomplished in stage two, "investigating needs," and stage three, " suggesting a course of action." The data gathered in both the original and subsequent studies demonstrated that the most powerful predictor of how a person prefers to be communicated with is consistent with their type preferences, especially in the areas of the functional pairs.

The functional pairs are described in more detail in *Introduction to Type®* (Myers 1998) and are summarized in Table 2.1. The table states that people with a preference for Sensing require firm facts. Those for whom Sensing is coupled with Thinking need to hear those facts in a logical cause-and-effect manner. On the other hand, when Sensing is combined with Feeling, the requirement is of a much more personal nature.

These differences are clearly illustrated in the data we have collected for health care situations. While the data will be shown in more detail later, a few examples are provided here to bring the theory to life. Respondents with preferences for Sensing and Thinking asked for health care professionals to use:

- Straightforward language – tell me why this happened
- Clear concise explanations and directions
- Straight talk – be honest, tell it like it is

The emphasis is analytical and non-personal.

Those with preferences for Sensing and Feeling needed practitioners to:

- Spend time with me, answering *all* questions
- Give all the facts, be sympathetic
- Show honesty, caring

The tone here is factual but personalized.

Look now at the columns in Table 2.1 which relate to Intuition.

*Table 2.1* Effects of combinations of Perception and Judgment*

| *People who prefer:* | *ST*<br>SENSING<br>+<br>THINKING | *SF*<br>SENSING<br>+<br>FEELING | *NF*<br>INTUITION<br>+<br>FEELING | *NT*<br>INTUITION<br>+<br>THINKING |
|---|---|---|---|---|
| *Focus their attention on:* | Facts | Facts | Possibilities | Possibilities |
| *Tend to become adept at:* | Applying facts and experience | Meeting the daily concerns of people | Understanding the aspirations of people | Developing theoretical concepts |
| *Solve problems by:* | A detached analysis of facts in a step-by-step process moving from cause to effect | A personal view of facts in a step-by-step process considering the value of the outcome | A personal view of possibilities in an insightful process considering the value of the outcome | An objective analysis of possibilities in an insightful process moving from cause to effect |

The Sensing, factual approach is replaced by a focus on "possibilities." As we have already seen, however, there is a further difference which depends upon the other preference, Feeling or Thinking.

Those with preferences for Intuition and Feeling are looking for a person-centered, individualized approach that matches their values. Intuitive Thinking types are more concerned with concepts and an analytical, cause-and-effect focus. These differences can be seen quite clearly in the following examples.

When asked what they thought was important in health care communication, Intuitive/Feeling types replied:

- Be empathetic, concerned with my state of being
- I need them to be gentle, compassionate but honest
- Tell me what the possibilities are, what my steps are
- Have patience, sit with me, stay nearby

The tone here is empathetic and personalized. The words used are often more conceptual – for example, "empathetic, compassionate."

Those with Intuitive/Thinking preferences asked for information in these terms:

- Clarity
- As much information about options as possible
- Give me my options and be prepared to discuss a course of action
- Straightforward facts with reasonable alternatives

The emphasis here is on options that make logical sense.

These short quotations help us to see the different needs of patients. They also begin to explain why it may be easier for us to deal with some people rather than others. If we happen to have a similar type preference, we may inadvertently match our patient's communication preferences.

The examples above begin to demonstrate in a relatively straightforward manner the value of functional pairs in health care communication. It may be helpful to look in more detail at some work that has been done in other contexts.

Pearman and Albritton (1997), in their aptly entitled book *I'm Not Crazy, I'm Just Not You,* describe the functional pairs as the "cognitive core" adding that:

> When all of the other preferred expressions of preferences fade, the habits of mind that result from the interactions of the mental

functions provide a bedrock on which you can build under-standing of each type's world view.

The term "bedrock" relates particularly well to FLEX Care since it not only reflects the fact that the functional pairs provide a solid foundation for understanding differences in communication, but also the fact that when health care professionals are talking to patients they are dealing with fundamental issues which may have deep and frightening implications.

The result of research undertaken by Pearman and Albritton is repro-duced in Table 2.2. Their data further describes the functional pairs. The objective, factual approach of Sensing and Thinking is reflected in the words "matter-of-fact," "practical" and "reasonable." For Sensing and Feeling, the focus on the "daily concerns of other people" is amplified by the phrases "seeks to meet needs" and "seen as compassionate" with an interest in "things concretely affecting others." Intuition and Feeling, the functional pair which seeks to understand people and their "aspira-tions" through an "insightful" process is described in Table 2.2 as being "aesthetic," "tender-minded" and "unconventional." Finally, Intuition and Thinking, the pair which sees the development of "theoretical con-cepts" as central, together with a tendency towards "objective analysis," is developed by the phrases "methodically attentive to theory, model," "ingenious" and "focuses on theoretical relationships."

Returning to the phrases "cognitive styles" and "cognitive core" it can be seen that the functional pairs do indeed address "bedrock" issues that are expressed in communication styles.

You may want to refer to Table 2.2 to further understand your own type preferences and think about situations when you commu-nicate with others in a different mode. Type differences can be extraordinarily useful in understanding more fully the diversity of reactions to a situation.

## Recognizing preference – behavior cues

In order to apply the concept of type to communication or practical influencing one needs to address how to "know" another's type. It is of course impractical to present an individual with a Myers-Briggs Type Indicator for completion and scoring before beginning to work together. It is also unnecessary. In contrast to determining one's own preference, as a baseline for how the world is approached, a FLEX practitioner, who is looking to understand others, needs to be aware of only two things. First, everyone uses all preferences at various

Table 2.2   The Cognitive Core*

**ST**
**Sensing with Thinking**
tough-minded
reasonable
matter-of-fact
practical
verifies facts – weighs, measures
orderly
self-controlled
self-satisfied
internally consistent

**NT**
**Intuition with Thinking**
psychologically minded
ingenious
analytical
focuses on theoretical relationships
likes autonomy
often clever
has defined interests
pride of objectivity
methodically attentive to theory, model

**SF**
**Sensing with Feeling**
factually oriented
gentle and modest
seeks to meet needs
expresses personal warmth
seen as compassionate
responsible
conscientious
patient with detail
focuses on things concretely affecting others

**NF**
**Intuition with Feeling**
tender-minded
enthusiastic
insightful
seeks new projects, complexity
flexible
identifies symbolic and theoretical relationships
aesthetic
inventive, non-conforming
unconventional thought processes

times. Second, observation of an individual's behavior cues will identify their "type mode" as it currently presents itself. The individual will almost always want to be dealt with as this type mode suggests. The overall aim is to understand the other person, gain perspective and FLEX in order to interact more effectively.

The simplicity and flexibility of FLEX Care can most easily be seen in practice. In order to bring the theory to life it may help you to think of individuals who most clearly exhibit the cues under discussion – just one note of caution: be sure to think of individuals you like or appreciate. No type preference is inherently bad or good. It would be a mistake to ascribe negative behaviors to any type.

The key to working successfully with FLEX Care is first to listen and observe the behavior cues of the other person and then match them. It helps to be aware of your own preferred behavior since this will make it easier for you to be aware of your own part in the communication. We will look at each of the basic aspects of type in turn (see Chapter 1 for a review of the four basic dimensions of type). We will use the Four-Part Framework terms for each of these dimensions because they often help to clarify the behaviors observed, and we will use the four-stage communication model to highlight which aspects of type are most important at a given time.

## Initiating the interaction

When initiating an interaction the scale which is most relevant to the exchange is that of Extraversion and Introversion. In "FLEX" language they are referred to as "Talk it Out" and "Think it Through." The behavior cues associated with these preferences are set out below. As in the previous chapter, you might like to hypothesize your own preferences and compare them with your original ideas.

| ☐ **Talk it Out** | ☐ **Think it Through** |
|---|---|
| Rapid speech | Pauses in giving information |
| Appears to "think aloud" | Quieter voice volume |
| Interrupts | Shorter sentences, not run on |
| Louder volume to voice | |

(FLEX Talk Brock Associates, 1991)

A group of health care professionals who were learning about FLEX Care for the first time were asked how they experienced these differences in terms of behavior. Responses included:

*Talk it Out*

- Immediate eye contact
- Tell you what they want, ask lots of questions, sometimes as they are walking in
- Make decisions right away, often change their mind
- Dominate the conversation

*Think it Through*

- Head down, no eye contact
- Wait to be asked in (don't barge in)
- Need time to think
- Slow-moving discussion
- Have to draw information from them

One person, with a "Think it Through" preference, added that patients who fell into the opposite category: ". . . make me nervous, I think 'Oh dear, they aren't going to listen. I will have to repeat what I say.'"

The group who tended to prefer the "Talk it Out" approach reported that when they were involved with patients who appeared to need to "Think it Through," they tended to:

- Just carry on
- Get frustrated
- Talk too much themselves to fill any gap in conversation

These are perfectly normal reactions and describe how communication can be affected by the interaction of different preferences. One other note can be made. Notice in the "Think it Through" example above, the phrase "don't barge in" was used by a Think-it-Througher about a Talk-it-Outer. This phrase has a slightly negative connotation. In talking or thinking about another person, if you find yourself using a slightly negatively connoted word, consider that you may be reacting to a type, or type mode, difference. You may find this a helpful signal or behavior cue for yourself.

## Investigating needs and Suggesting a course of action

Once a degree of personal rapport has been reached the next step is to discover what the needs are. The scales which relate most closely to discovering needs are Sensing (Specifics) and Intuition (Big Picture) and Thinking (Logical Implications) and Feeling (Impact on People). We will take each of these in turn in order to examine the behavior cues associated with each. Hypothesize your own preferences and compare them with your original ideas about your type preference from Chapter 1.

| ☐ **Specifics** | ☐ **Big Picture** |
|---|---|
| Asks for step-by-step information or instruction | Asks for the current and long-range implications |
| Asks "what," "how" questions | Asks "why" questions |
| Uses precise descriptions | Talks in general terms |
| Interested in practical applications | Interested in possibilities |

(FLEX Talk, Brock Associates, 1991)

Again, a group of health care professionals, who were learning about FLEX Care for the first time, were asked how they experienced this aspect in practice. Responses included patients asking:

### Specifics

- What material will you use?
- How long will it be before I can eat?
- Do I need an injection?
- How long will the treatment last?

Notice the initial concerns expressed in "What" and " How" questions focused on establishing the facts of the immediate situation.

### Big Picture

- Will I always have my treatment here?
- Are there any alternative treatments for this condition? Do you use laser?
- Can you treat the rest of my family?
- Why can't I find information about this treatment on the Internet?

Notice the initial concerns expressed in "Why" questions, looking for possibilities and new options.

Practitioners with a preference for "Specifics" tended to experience patients with behavior cues related to the "Big Picture" as being uncommitted to treatment, since they did not ask what appeared to be the relevant questions. Practitioners with a preference for the "Big Picture" felt threatened and de-skilled by too many factual questions.

The scale of Thinking and Feeling also comes into play in the stages of investigating needs and suggesting a course of action. In "FLEX" language these dimensions are referred to as "Logical Implications" and "Impact on People." The behavior cues associated with these preferences are presented below. As before, hypothesize your own preferences and compare them with your original ideas from Chapter 1.

| ☐ Logical Implications | ☐ Impact on People |
|---|---|
| Appears to be "testing you" or your knowledge" | Strives for harmony in interaction |
| Weighs objective evidence | May talk about what they value |
| Not impressed that others have decided in favor | Asks how others acted/resolved the situation |
| Conversations follow a pattern of "if this, then that" | Matters to them whether others have been taken into account |

(FLEX Talk, Brock Associates, 1991)

The group of health care professionals who were learning about FLEX Care for the first time were asked how they experienced these differences in practice. Responses about patients included:

*Logical Implications*

- Complain
- Praise only for competence
- Process has to be logical
- Less expressive/emotional
- Task before social

*Impact on People*

- Smile/friendly
- Wouldn't complain directly (may do to someone else)
- Ingratiating
- Warm
- Stroking behaviors/massages your ego
- Flattering

The group with a Thinking preference found patients with Feeling preferences to be "pathetic, uncomplicated, non-threatening and annoying." Those with a Feeling preference, on the other hand, found patients with a Thinking preference to be "arrogant, rude/pushy, and apparently inflexible."

These comments are much more critical than those we have read so far. This is not an uncommon reaction. Type provides a framework for understanding these negative reactions in a way that often defuses them.

## Next step or closing

Having completed the first three steps, we now approach the time to complete the exchange. The scale which comes into play at this stage is that of Judging and Perceiving. In "FLEX" language these aspects of type are referred to as "Joy of Closure" and "Joy of Processing." The behavior cues associated with these preferences are present below. Hypothesize your own preferences and compare them with your original ideas from Chapter 1.

| ☐ **Joy of Closure** | ☐ **Joy of Processing** |
|---|---|
| Moves to closure | Be ready for spontaneity |
| Works to accomplish goals | Moves in desired direction |
| Wants a known structure and to stick with it | "Goals" are seen as confining |
| Interested in the end product of our work, the result | Interested in how we work, the process |

(FLEX Talk, Brock Associates, 1991)

A group of health care professionals, who were learning about FLEX Care for the first time, were asked how they experienced this aspect in practice. Responses included patients asking:

### *Joy of Closure*

- How long will it take?
- How long will it last?
- Guarantees?
- Is there a six-month recall?
- How soon will I get the results?

These comments all relate to structuring the situation and getting an end result.

## *Joy of Processing*

- Forget appointments or are late
- Laid-back approach
- You can get away with taking a short cut
- Don't mind inconvenience
- Need more time to decide
- Tend to lose important pieces of paper
- Don't always read information

These comments all relate to the process of working together, not the end result.

Those with a Perceiving preference reported feeling inadequate and inefficient when treating patients with a Judging preference, but said "at least they pay and don't forget appointments." Those with a Judging preference felt they could get away with things with patients with a preference for Perceiving because they didn't always notice!

We have now looked at each scale and matched it to a stage in the communication process. It is important to note at this stage, however, that communication is fluid rather than compartmentalized. We need to remember, therefore, that throughout the discussion there will be a tendency for some patients to talk, while others think. Additionally, some will be seeking an answer at an early stage while others want to weigh options for some time. However, recognizing these fundamental steps is essential to understanding how to FLEX with one's patients.

## Putting FLEX Care into action

We have just looked at the impact of each type dimension independently in order to give straightforward examples of type preference in action. However, as previously stated, the data shows that the functional pairs best differentiate communication styles and requirements. People with differing functional preferences seem to use different words or different dialects.

When asked "How do you want to be treated in a health care situation?" communication styles preferred by people with different functional preferences fell into the same well-recognized patterns as were previously seen in general communication settings.

In a health care setting, those who prefer *Specifics/Logical Implications (ST)* say their preferences for communication are:

*   Be knowledgeable, efficient, competent, pay attention to detail
*   Understand my needs
*   Give me time to absorb events

Those who prefer *Specifics/Impact on People (SF)* say their preferences for communication in a health care setting are:

*   Be friendly, caring, cheerful
*   Listen to me
*   Treat me as a person (possibly "known" by name to the professional)
*   Ensure privacy
*   Be efficient

Those who prefer *Big Picture/Impact on People (NF)* say their preferences for communication in a health care setting are:

*   Treat me as an individual
*   Respect my view, involve me
*   Be kind, sympathetic
*   Be professional, that is, listen to me

Those who prefer *Big Picture/Logical Implications (NT)* say their preferences for communication in a health care setting are:

*   Be professional
*   Respect my intelligence
*   Involve me in decisions, offer alternatives
*   Treat me as a competent person

More generally, the data revealed some words and phrases which are characteristic of certain type preferences. The word "empathy" is often and spontaneously used by NF types. It is sometimes used by NT types but rarely by Sensing types. The word "relationship" is also used by those with an Intuitive preference and fits into a pattern often seen with Intuitive types – if a word is longer, Intuitives tend to use it. Sensing types tend to use words and phrases which are more down to earth. For example, STs and SFs are more likely to say "get to know me" than "build a relationship."

One word used by all types is "listen." When individuals are asked about what they want or need in a health care situation, "listen" seems to rise to the level of a plea. It appears more often than any other word in the FLEX data. Different types have different understandings of what listening means, but one thing is certain: if we listen closely for behavior cues and then respond using a matching "dialect" the patient will know that we *listened and heard.*

## Matching communications

Having read about these differences the next question is "Yes, but what exactly do I do?"

Table 2.3 provides information about the considerable differences in the preferences of patients with differing functional pairs. It is particularly valuable to compare those with the greatest differences, ST and NF, SF and NT.

It can be seen that for STs the focus is on the facts, well-ordered and delivered with the minimum of fuss. The NFs priority is to be seen as an individual with complex personal needs. SFs place the highest value on a caring, personal service, while the NTs seek recognition of their intelligence and demonstration of competence by the professional with whom they are working.

Having now introduced the theory and provided a wide range of examples it may be helpful for you to complete a set of exercises before moving on to the next chapter presents examples taken from both health care professionals and patients.

## Exercises

1   Reflect first on what you have learned about your own preferences. Then reflect on anyone close to you who might exemplify each of the eight basic aspects of type, given the behavior cues you have observed. Remember, only use individuals you like or appreciate for your examples. There are no good or bad preferences. Make a note of any examples before reading the next chapter.

2   Think of an example where you were a patient and you felt the communication went well. Can you identify behaviors in the professional that matched your own preferences?

3   Now think of an example where you were the patient and the communication did not go well. Can you identify behaviors in the professional that did not match your own preferences?

*Table 2.3*  "To do's" for type modes in health care settings*

| ST – Facts with practicality | SF – Personal service |
|---|---|
| • Be brief, give concise facts<br>• Be straightforward and honest<br>• Know the facts about my condition and expect to be questioned on them<br>• Give me information on the specific treatment options so I can weigh them<br>• Present the information in a logical way, do not go off on a tangent<br>• Give me factual written information about my condition/treatment<br>• Have available percentages or relevant data for comparison and information<br>• Expect to be "tested" | • Listen carefully to me, give me your time and complete attention<br>• Be warm and friendly<br>• Give me factual information honestly, but with a personal touch – for example, remember what I've already told you<br>• Provide practical information and examples about my condition<br>• Tell me about other people who have had the same treatment<br>• Explain any options clearly and allow me time to decide |
| NF – Supporting the vision | NT – Logical options with competence |
| • Treat me with respect, as a whole person, not a case number<br>• Listen to and value my concerns<br>• Provide overall solutions, an overview without details<br>• Take time to discuss my concerns, be honest but kind<br>• Know that my case is unique to me<br>• Be sincere<br>• Get to know me as a person<br>• I may want to discuss alternatives or complementary treatments; take this seriously | • Respect my intelligence and my need to understand<br>• Demonstrate your competence<br>• Answer my questions in an honest, open way – do not hide anything<br>• Give me overall options so I can see a pattern<br>• Be informed about new alternative treatments<br>• Listen to my views, ask before giving advice<br>• Do not expect/assume a personal relationship – that will be built when competence is shown<br>• Show that you continually update your knowledge |

*Adapted from *To Do's for Type Modes in Health Care Settings* © Judy Allen and Susan A. Brock 1999. Reprinted with permission.

4   Think of an example where you feel your own preferences helped in communication where you were the professional, and one where they did not.

## Summary

In this chapter we have introduced data which shows how different types want their communication. The data from health care situations paralleled data from more general influencing situations. These data have been used as the basis for FLEX Care – a practical system of understanding and responding to patients in health care situations.

Examples of behavior cues showing type mode were presented. In addition, specific ways to respond to individuals in various type modes were highlighted.

In the next chapter we will present a series of case studies provided by both health care professionals and patients. These will provide an opportunity for you to apply your understanding of the type theory to real situations.

# 3   Seeing type preference in action

## How can I use this framework as I work in my setting?

The first two chapters have set out the basic theory contained within the Myers-Briggs Type Indicator (MBTI) and the FLEX Care model. Often people learn a great deal about application of the MBTI by attending seminars. This chapter will, however, provide a different opportunity for you to apply what you have learned. Case studies of actual patients or professionals will describe incidents in the individual's own words. You will be able to use the cues given for type preference to analyze the type mode of the individual. A discussion of each case will follow to verify your own analysis.

Many professionals find that their first step in using the type framework in their setting is simply to become aware of type differences: "Not everybody wants what I would want in a health care situation." The second step is to keep doing what you are doing, if it is working. If it is not, or not working as well as you would like, the third step is to ask yourself four questions to help identify the patient's type mode and better match it.

Ask yourself, "Is this person:"

- Using "Talk it Out" (Extraversion) or "Think it Through" (Introversion)?
- Focusing on "Specifics" (Sensing) or "Big Picture" (Intuition)?
- Analyzing using "Logical Implications" (Thinking) or "Impact on People" (Feeling)?
- Concerned with structuring to get to the "Joy of Closure" (Judging) or interested in the "Joy of Processing" (Perceiving)?

One clue to a possible type difference between your type preference and the patient's type mode is if you find yourself using a negatively connoted word or phrase to describe the patient. For example, "She's a know it all" or "He's bossy." Type differences are not the only source of these internal comments but often type can provide a perspective and make a potentially negative interaction more positive.

## Gathering data using the Critical Incident Technique

The case study interviews were conducted using the "Critical Incident Technique" framework. The overall aim of the interviews was to elicit stories relating to communication in health care settings, some which worked well and some which worked less well. Both professional health care workers and patients were interviewed. All those interviewed had verified their MBTI type.

This method of collecting information was first developed in the Second World War by John Flanagan. He was asked to help select and train air crews for the British Royal Air Force. Flanagan felt that assessments of the trainee pilots at that time were vague and as such would not yield the specific training competencies demanded for dangerous work. Flanagan issued a questionnaire to flight instructors and pilots which asked for specifics such as "the last time you saw a trainee do something that was effective/ineffective . . . What led up to the situation . . . What did he do?" This technique is now called Critical Incident Technique. The fields of social science and health care have adopted it to gather data about behaviors critical to professional competence.

The value of using this approach in health care lies in the ability to learn about how people actually apply their professional expertise in practice. If they are simply asked, for example, "How would you conduct an interview with a patient who has just received a frightening diagnosis?" the response would be likely to reflect what they imagine they would, or should, do – so-called espoused theory.

Spencer and Spencer (1993) designed a set of questions that reflect the Critical Incident Technique for what they called the "Behavioral Event Interview." They believe that this process provides a true picture of what people actually do, which "gets behind" what people say they do. The questions are as follows:

1   What was the situation? What events led up to it?
2   Who was involved?
3   What did you think, feel or want to do in the situation?
4   What did you actually do or say?
5   What was the outcome? What happened?

This particular set of questions was used to obtain all the cases used in this chapter. The main advantage of using this technique, in addition to providing a clear focus for the narrative, is to capture the respondent's thoughts, actions and feelings in their own words. These are key elements from which type mode can be deduced.

All those interviewed, both patients and professionals, were asked to relate two stories, one in which communication was seen to go well and one in which it did not. They were given a choice as to the order in which they related their stories. Interestingly, overall those with a preference for Thinking tended to start with a negative story while those with Feeling preferences tended to focus first on the positive story. For clarity, all cases will be presented with the positive incident first.

## Working with the interview material

Working with these stories will help you to recognize differences in type language and begin to pick out behavior cues related to type mode. As you read, note the possible type elements. Use both the list of general type behavior cues set out in Table 3.1 and also the specific list that precedes each set of critical incidents, as a guide. When you study the table, it is important to remember that type mode cues are present throughout the whole interaction. However, as we meet our patient we often first notice the cues of Extraversion and Introversion. As the interaction progresses and we begin to investigate needs and suggest action, the functional pairs – that is how the person wants to take in information and come to a conclusion – become most important. Throughout the interaction, but especially as we draw to a close, cues of Judging or Perceiving are key.

The incidents will be presented in four sections representing the four functional pairs:

Sensing and Thinking        (ST)
Sensing and Feeling         (SF)
Intuition and Feeling       (NF)
Intuition and Thinking      (NT)

All incidents relate to health care situations from either the patient's or the health care professional's point of view. Each individual's incident will then be followed by a short section in which we will discuss the language or cues that indicate type mode.

*Table 3.1* Identifying behavior cues – what will I see?*

| STAGES OF INTERACTION | CLIENT'S TYPE MODE | |
|---|---|---|
| **Meeting or beginning an interaction** | **TALK IT OUT (E – Extraversion)**<br>• higher energy and animation<br>• faster pace<br>• more words rather than less | **THINK IT THROUGH (I – Introversion)**<br>• more measured pace, pauses<br>• quieter, more considered approach<br>• less words, rather than more |
| **Investigating needs**<br><br>**and**<br><br>**Suggesting action** | **SPECIFICS/LOGICAL OPTIONS (ST – Sensing and Thinking)**<br>• values factual information<br>• gives the facts in a logical order<br>• practical "let's get the task done" approach<br>• interested in tried and trusted methods with data back-up | **SPECIFICS/IMPACT ON PEOPLE (SF – Sensing and Feeling)**<br>• seeks a personalized service, a caring relationship<br>• asks for facts rather than theory<br>• wants a warm and friendly approach<br>• interest in whatever worked for others |
| | **BIG PICTURE/LOGICAL OPTIONS (NT – Intuition and Thinking)**<br>• asks for logical options<br>• tests practitioner's competence<br>• interested in cutting-edge methods | **BIG PICTURE/IMPACT ON PEOPLE (NF – Intuition and Feeling)**<br>• sees their situation as unique<br>• needs to be valued as a person<br>• interested in new methods especially those that focus on the whole person |
| **Pacing to closure**<br><br>**or**<br><br>**Next steps** | **JOY OF CLOSURE (J – Judging)**<br>• goal-oriented<br>• moves the conversation toward closure or next step<br>• irritated by waiting | **JOY OF PROCESSING (P – Perceiving)**<br>• process-oriented<br>• adopts a spontaneous approach<br>• mentions issues along the way, thus may appear to go off track<br>• takes action at the "last minute" |

*Adapted for FLEX Care®, 1999 and from "FLEX Selling®/FLEX Talk® Four-Part Framework© WHAT DO YOU SEE AND HEAR?" 1990 Brock Associates. Revised 1995. Reprinted with permission.

You will see from the case histories that it is often easier to identify the cues relating to the functions than those relating to the Extravert/Introvert and Judging/Perceiving dimensions. In terms of the E/I dimension it is easier to "see" the cues in real life where pace and body language are observable. This is true to an extent for J/P too, particularly in relation to body language where, for example, impatience and a wish to achieve closure may be evident to the observer and may not transfer to the written word.

## SENSING AND THINKING

### ISTJ professional: Sue, chemotherapy nurse specialist

In the ensuing case study look for the following evidence of the professional's preferences:

**Introversion (I):**
(i)  Speaking with pauses
(ii) Preference for thinking through a situation before it occurs

**Sensing and Thinking (ST):**
(i)   Taking action based on " if . . . then" logic
(ii)  Giving step-by-step directions
(iii) Wanting or having specific data
(iv) Using straightforward communication

**Judging (J):**
(i)  Preferring to structure a situation
(ii) Methodically assuming an outcome

---

### Positive critical incident

**1 What was the situation? What events led up to it?**
A bereaved relative came to our oncology unit, the daughter of a patient we had treated. I had never met her and he hadn't talked about her. She came in to make a donation. Although she had booked an appointment, I had forgotten it and I was busy – I hadn't really prepared myself.

**2 Who was involved?**
Me, the woman and her grown-up daughter.

**3 What did you think, feel or want to do in the situation?**
Initially I thought "I don't want to do this, I don't want to face her." I just knew I had to.

**4 What did you actually do or say?**
For a few moments, I finished off what I was doing, even though it wasn't important. I then took her to a quiet room and introduced myself. We talked about her father and that he had died suddenly of an unrelated illness, pneumonia. I said that I was so upset about this, about him dying so suddenly after undergoing all the treatment for cancer – that it seemed so unfair. She actually finished off my sentence then, agreeing with me. I decided to tell her that he had been the life and soul of the party while having chemotherapy, how everyone looked forward to seeing him. I related some funny incidents that happened while he came to us and she could relate this to her father's personality, her knowledge of him. I gave her a picture of how he coped with his treatment away from them.

**5 What was the outcome? What happened?**
I felt she could take these incidents away with her and use them in her own grief process by retelling them to other people. It helped me to be able to talk to her, to meet her, it rounded the story up for me.

**Negative critical incident**

**1 What was the situation? What events led up to it?**
A young man was dying of cancer, he and his wife had both accepted the fact that he was going to die – and he had made his mind up that he wanted to die in the hospital ward that was known to him. I was his main nurse carer. He had also expressed the fact that he didn't want to die alone in a side room.

**2 Who was involved?**
Me, the patient, his wife and a night duty nurse.

**3 What did you think, feel or want to do in the situation?**
I thought that, because it was the last thing he would request, it should be honored, it was the least thing we could do.

**4 What did you actually do or say?**
I handed this information to the night shift – on the night we expected him to die – both verbally and in written form. I went off duty in all good faith, thinking this would be honored.

**5 What was the outcome? What happened?**
When I came back next morning, the nurse said that they had had to move him into a side room and he was dying. When I challenged her reason for moving him, she didn't answer with any logic at all, she just said "we always move dying patients into side rooms." I talked it over with her, she said she did read what I had written but felt as he was unconscious, it didn't matter,

*Noting the behavior cues*

**Introversion (I):**
(i)   At one point Sue said that the relative had finished her sentence off for her, indicating a pause (or that the relative was in Extravert mode and interrupted).
(ii)  Sue expressed unease at having to face a relative unprepared.
(iii) Sue took time to finish off an unimportant task as a way to give herself time to gather her thoughts.

**Sensing and Thinking (ST):**
(i)   Sue noted that if she gave the relative certain information, she could use it in her grieving process. This is the use of the facts for a logical purpose.
(ii)  The manner in which Sue shared her sadness about the way in which the patient had died was direct, as was her expression of her feeling that it was "unfair," not, for example, "heart wrenching."
(iii) She left step-by-step written directions for the care of the dying patient.

(iv) Logic – *if* it was the man's last request, *then* we should honor it, even if it is an unusual practice.

## Judging (J):
(i)   Sue was initially uneasy because she had forgotten the relative was coming and was not prepared.
(ii)  She also expressed appreciation that meeting the patient's daughter "rounded the story up for me."
(iii) Sue put all possible arrangements in place to meet the patient's request, that is she structured it. She could not understand why the plan was not followed.

## ISTP patient: Zoe, classical music retailer

In the ensuing case study look for the following evidence of the patient's preferences:

## Introversion (I):
(i)  Preference for thinking the situation through
(ii) Allowing others to take the lead in talking

## Sensing and Thinking (ST):
(i)   Seeking factual information
(ii)  Needing relevant data
(iii) Appreciating honesty, good skills and straightforward conversation

## Perceiving (P):
(i)  Keeping options open
(ii) "No decision before it's time." Closure isn't a source of satisfaction. A good look at all the facts and options is satisfying.

---

### Positive critical incident

#### 1 What was the situation?
I had an early breast cancer, no lumps, just cells contained. At the time there was a trial where, if you went in for it you either had radiotherapy, a specialist drug, nothing or a combination of treatments. It was a trial for this sort of cancer, very specific. Initially there was a lot of pressure to go into the

trial, which caused us quite a lot of angst. We asked to see the consultant and read all the information.

## 2 Who was involved?
My husband, the consultant and me.

## 3 What did you think, feel or want to do in the situation?
I felt guilty about not wanting to do the trial but I didn't want to. I felt I was well, there was a very low risk and if I got the short straw, i.e. combination, that would be too much. I felt annual monitoring would be enough. If it recurred, we could always think again. I hoped the consultant would say, "No, you're quite right, you don't need any treatment, you'd be better to leave it."

## 4 What did you actually do or say?
My husband did all the talking, he is very good at technicalities and analysis. We were there for an hour, everything we asked the consultant answered as honestly as possible. We tried to get him to say, "If it weren't for this trial what treatment would you recommend?" He said, "I honestly don't know, the trial is set up to establish the best treatment." He didn't flannel. My husband asked if I would be foolish not to have treatment and he said, "You have to make the decision." We discussed all the facts, recurrences, etc.

## 5 What was the outcome? What happened?
We said we felt awkward about not supporting the trial but we felt on balance the risk of feeling worse for a long time wasn't worth it. He said, "Fine." We made a clinical judgment for ourselves. He did not put pressure on us, which was right. He was supportive and just gave us the facts. It was all factual and useful.

## Negative critical incident

### 1 What was the situation?

I had a miscarriage and follow-up treatment. Three months later I had a violent hemorrhage – it was very dramatic. I don't usually panic but I thought I was going to die. I went to hospital by ambulance and the staff were good. It settled down and I waited to see the doctor.

### 2 Who was involved?

Just me and the doctor.

### 3 What did you think, feel or want to do in the situation?

I was really frightened.

### 4 What did you actually do or say?

He just dismissed it. Even though it was nearly twenty years ago I remember what he said exactly, "You women, a thimble full of blood and you think it's the end." He then said, "We'd better look at you, then."

### 5 What was the outcome? What happened?

I knew it was serious, I had had one before, and he treated it as though it was just a little bit of blood. He trivialized it, not to make me feel better but because he was dismissive. It was a nightmare, I did not need him to be sympathetic, just aware that I wasn't making a fuss.

## *Noting the behavior cues*

### Introversion (I):

(i) Zoe and her husband read as much information as they could before seeing the consultant.
(ii) She let her husband do the talking.
(iii) Zoe did not recollect speaking to the doctor who she felt treated her so badly.

### Sensing and Thinking (ST):

(i) In the discussion relating to breast cancer, Zoe used the words "fact" or "factual" a great deal.

(ii) She was clearly asking for specific options.
(iii) She appreciated the consultant being "straightforward and honest."
(iv) Zoe was aware that the doctor treating her hemorrhage dismissed her even though she knew the facts and had made an accurate comparison to past experience.

**Perceiving (P):**
(i) Zoe looked at and discussed a variety of options.
(ii) She needed to consider and discuss all the options concerning the cancer before reaching a decision, i.e. "No decision before it's time." Pressure caused her "angst."
(iii) It's possible to reconsider the decision on treatment for breast cancer, "If it recurred, we could always think again."


## SENSING AND FEELING

### ISFJ professional: John, osteopath

In the ensuing case study look for the following evidence of the professional's experience:

**Introversion (I):**
(i) Calm manner
(ii) Thinks treatment through carefully

**Sensing and Feeling (SF):**
(i) Personalized approach
(ii) Wanting to be of practical help
(iii) Clear explanations
(iv) Listening carefully

**Judging (J):**
(i) Structured approach
(ii) Outcome planned

## Positive critical incident

### 1 What was the situation?
A new patient came with sub-acute back pain. He was visiting friends in this area. He was staying with a local doctor who booked him in. The patient was due to drive home the following day. He appeared quite nervous when he arrived.

### 2 Who was involved?
Me and the patient.

### 3 What did you think, feel or want to do in the situation?
I felt fairly confident that we would be able to develop a rapport where he was comfortable with me, whereby I could give him (a) treatment and (b) advice. I wanted to make him more comfortable and confident about his journey home. I knew he saw an osteopath at home. I realized, however, that his expectation of one session might be initially a little high.

### 4 What did you actually do or say?
He gave me his history and before I treated him I did say that I thought I could be of some help but that I would be guarded because of the need for him to drive the next day – that he would be pretty sore if we did too much. I examined him, he was very apprehensive, I could feel his fear and he was sweating a great deal – and apologizing for this. He slightly exaggerated his pain. I laid him down and examined him and explained what I thought had gone on. (I do this because it helps people to know I've heard what they have been telling me.) I said I could make him more comfortable and he could see his "friendly osteopath" after he got home. I feel this matched his expectations with what I could achieve.

### 5 What was the outcome, what happened?
Afterwards he relaxed and seemed happy with what I had done. I was sure that he felt some immediate benefit. He wrote later thanking me for my "excellent" help and said that though the problem was not completely resolved the "discomfort was so much less" after treatment. He added that he could stand up straight!

## Negative critical incident

### 1 What was the situation? What events led up to it?

A new patient came with upper back and neck pain. She had a six-month-old baby and was breast-feeding. I was taking a case history and was trying to open things up, as I sensed that building rapport might be difficult. I wanted her to be able to talk to me easily. She was fairly monosyllabic, I asked open questions and she replied "yes" or "no" – she wasn't picking up on that. A friend had recommended that she come and see me. Quite early on she told me that she didn't like treatment that involved touch.

### 2 Who was involved?

Me and the patient.

### 3 What did you think, feel or want to do in the situation?

I felt there was a mix of factors. She was quite stressed and seemed to have a lack of insight into the need to look for causes of her discomfort – she just felt that the pain was unjust, seemed a bit angry, "why me?" I knew it wasn't going to be easy, my mind was working overtime, trying my best to know how to help. I did however think I could help – and that I would break the ice.

### 4 What did you actually do or say?

Having taken the history, I left the room while she removed her blouse – having explained that I needed to see the top part of her back. When I come back into the room at this stage, I often ask a question, to distract the patient in case they feel embarrassed. I did this but got little response. I then asked where it hurt and did a series of movements. I then put my hands on her back and I explained everything I was doing, but got no reply and no eye contact. I went out of my way to make things as little interventionist as I could. She lay pretty much rigid.

### 5 What was the outcome? What happened?

I persevered, told her what I had found, and what treatment was needed. I checked her understanding and she said she did understand, but without much conviction. I did some treatment – she never relaxed. I decided that was all I could do that day and told her that I would need to see her two or three times more. She made little response, did arrange a follow-up appointment which she later cancelled. In hindsight, I feel I could have mentioned that the treatment would involve touch but I thought I would be able to relax her.

## Noting the behavior cues

### Introversion (I):
(i) The tone of both consultations is measured, even when things are difficult.
(ii) John demonstrated his ability to listen by specifically mentioning ways in which he consciously lets his patients know that he has heard them.

### Sensing and Feeling (SF):
(i) John placed great emphasis on the need to build a rapport and found it hard when he could not do this.
(ii) He was aware that the first patient had to drive the next day and took that into account when treating him.
(iii) In both cases he described the nature of the treatment very carefully.

### Judging (J):
(i) John's accounts of the way in which he treats his patients demonstrate a carefully planned, step-by-step approach.
(ii) In both cases, he had an outcome planned at an early stage. In the first case the patient should be able to drive and in the second he would establish a rapport.

## ISFP patient: George, farm manager

In the ensuing case study look for the following evidence of the patient's preferences:

### Introversion (I):
(i) Keeping to oneself, not "talking things out" initially

**Sensing and Feeling (SF):**
(i)   Personal caring, family support/inclusion
(ii)  Personal relationships are important
(iii) Fact-based questions, not theoretical

**Perceiving (P):**
(i)  Letting things take their course
(ii) Not taking action until "it's time"

---

## Positive critical incident

### 1 What was the situation?

I had had pains in my chest and I had had them for four months. I was managing a busy farm and was very tired. I hadn't told anyone about the pains. I thought they would go away and it was nothing to worry about. When they didn't go away I decided to go to my doctor and get it checked out.

### 2 Who was involved?

Me and my doctor.

### 3 What did you think, feel or want to do in the situation?

I was worried, it was not an excruciating pain but I wanted to find out what was wrong with me.

### 4 What did you actually do or say?

When I explained the symptoms he examined me and he said "I think it's possibly angina and I'd like you to have some tests."

### 5 What was the outcome?

He actually contacted the hospital and said he wanted me to have tests. He also said he was worried because he hadn't seen me for such a long time and farmers were usually very fit. He was extremely nice about it. It helped that he lived on the farming estate where I worked and I knew him, that helped. It was easier to go to someone I knew. I found him approachable and down-to-earth – I felt he would do as much as he could for me.

**Negative critical incident**

**1 What was the situation? What events led up to it?**
I was having investigations and had agreed with the charge nurse that my wife would be allowed to come in when I was given the results. The tests were crucial as I had a heart condition.

**2 Who was involved?**
Me, the nurse, my wife and the cardiologist.

**3 What did you think, feel or want to do in the situation?**
I wanted my wife to be there so she could ask more questions, as I might not be in a fit state to ask.

**4 What did you actually do or say?**
I asked the nurse to make sure my wife was called in when the doctor came. My wife also asked and she promised she would do that. The nurse concerned went off to lunch, forgetting to tell her colleagues about us, so my wife was not there when I got my results.

**5 What was the outcome? What happened?**
In actual fact, the condition was far more serious than first we thought. We were both angry and upset because my wife had been waiting and then wasn't called in. We didn't get enough information. I needed her there for personal support and information.

*Noting the behavior cues*

**Introversion (I):**
(i)   George had had chest pain and tiredness for some months before he told anyone.

**Sensing and Feeling (SF):**
(i)   George needed his wife to be with him when the results of his tests were explained and was very upset when this did not occur.
(ii)  It was particularly important to him that he "knew" the doctor and that he found him "approachable."

(iii) George focused on the symptoms in his first consultation and stressed the need for getting "enough information" in the second incident.

**Perceiving (P):**
(i)  George allowed the condition to run on for quite a while before seeking help.
(ii) He only went to the doctor when the symptoms did not go away.

## INTUITION AND FEELING

### ENFP professional: David, senior nurse, oncology

In the ensuing case study look for the following evidence of the professional's preferences:

**Extraversion (E):**
(i)  Using more words rather than less

**Intuition and Feeling (NF):**
(i)   Treating the patient as a whole person
(ii)  Identifying areas of distress
(iii) Wanting to communicate on a personal level
(iv)  Less interested in facts, more interested in the overall impact on the person
(v)   Talking in metaphors
(vi)  Using theoretical or complex words versus common everyday words

**Perceiving (P):**
(i)   Focus on the wider issues
(ii)  Leaving things open-ended
(iii) Focus on process (*how* things are going) versus focus on outcome (*what* is the result)

---

### Positive critical incident

**1 What was the situation? What events led up to it?**
I was seeing a sixty-year-old man with bowel cancer, with spread to the liver, and now with more generalized disease,

six months after the diagnosis. He was seeing the doctor to discuss stopping chemotherapy – we wanted to stop treatment because a bone scan indicated advancing disease. He also had back pain. Immediately before I saw him, the doctor had told him he was to stop chemotherapy.

**2 Who was involved?**
Me, the patient and his wife.

**3 What did you think, feel or want to do in the situation?**
I felt his pain was not just physical and I wanted to ease his distress. I had felt he had been in pain, total pain by which I mean – the anxiety. It is like a man looking over an abyss – at that point what you want to do is help someone not by saying "it's not there" but by saying "I believe it is there and I believe you can cope with that knowledge." This is because I think that existential abyss, where at some point we all reach that point where we say "I am going to die" and the majority of people can cope with that. I wanted to communicate on a deeper level than we'd been able to and to reassure him that whatever he felt it was all right to feel and say whatever he wanted to. In a physical sense, I wanted him to feel more comfortable.

**4 What did you actually do or say?**
He came in with his wife and I asked him to tell me his story, even though I had seen him at diagnosis. I wanted his story from the "this was how I felt, thought" perspective – not "I had this test and this was the result." Having asked him, I remained silent, I listened and then prompted gently from time to time to discover what was important to him. I asked, "What's really bothering you?" He focused on his sadness that chemo wasn't working. I then empathized (by empathized I mean – not being in his shoes because I can't be – but my linking the situation and the feeling it provokes) by saying "you feel sad and the chemotherapy isn't working, am I hearing you right?"

**5 What was the outcome? What happened?**
He began to cry and said he'd felt heard. We were then able to put that down and deal with the physical thing. He said

himself "we can move on from here." His wife said later that it also enabled them to talk about things together, more openly than before.

---

## Negative critical incident

**1 What was the situation? What events led up to it?**
This is about the same man just after he was diagnosed. He had been told fairly bluntly that he had liver disease and was going to die and would need to see a palliative care nurse. I was asked to go and see him, they told me he was stunned.

**2 Who was involved?**
Me and the patient.

**3 What did you think, feel or want to do in the situation?**
I wanted to get him to tell his story, so he would understand it and so that we could talk about follow-up care, what we could and couldn't do.

**4 What did you actually do or say?**
When I saw him, he was not so much stunned as in total denial. I gave him the opportunity to discuss his story – he did not want to talk about it. I suggested it was OK to be stunned and upset, he gave monosyllabic answers and looked close to tears but said "I'm not bloody upset" – in a very upset way.

**5 What was the outcome? What happened?**
All I was able to do was give him permission to deny his distress, I wouldn't push it further. I gave him a contact number to call me if he wanted to.

---

*Noting the behavior cues*

**Extraversion (E):**
(i)   In the positive incident, David used many words to describe the situation.

**Intuition and Feeling (NF):**
(i)   At an early stage, David wanted to hear the patient's story, to get to know about him rather than his illness.
(ii)  David was conscious of the patient's inner distress and wanted to help him to recognize it and express it.
(iii) He wanted the patient to share "his story" so that they could get to know each other before addressing the physical issues.
(iv)  David explained that initially he was not interested in test results.
(v)   He used complex words and metaphors – "that existential abyss."

**Perceiving (P):**
(i)   There was no initial plan, the conversation started with the need for David to hear the patient's story.
(ii)  After the first meeting, David left his contact number but did not press the patient to arrange a further meeting.
(iii) David expressed discomfort over the patient simply being told an outcome ("he had liver cancer and was going to die") – not leaving things open-ended or explaining the process of care.

## ENFJ patient: Mary, managing director

In the ensuing case study look for the following evidence of the patient's preferences:

**Extraversion (E):**
(i)   Talking things out

**Intuition and Feeling (NF):**
(i)   Wanting a positive relationship, a sense of equal partnership
(ii)  Looking for alternative options, treating the whole person
(iii) Reacting against being treated impersonally or as "lesser" than

**Judging (J):**
(i)   Emphasis on time
(ii)  Focus on outcome or clear plan of action

## Positive critical incident

**1 What was the situation? What events led up to it?**
I visited a medical herbalist one Saturday at a new center.

**2 Who was involved?**
The herbalist, a student and me.

**3 What did you think, feel or want to do in the situation?**
I had felt unwell for some time, and my work is very draining. I sometimes feel burnt out. I wanted to talk to someone who was interested in me, would be understanding but also knew what they were talking about.

**4 What did you actually do or say?**
I was asked if I minded being a guinea pig as he was training students. I was there an hour. They took a full medical history, urine sample, and examination of lymph glands, palpation of stomach and liver. I felt I was listened to, could ask questions. The medical training and knowledge of the herbalist were impressive. They prescribed herbs, but we also talked about diet and lifestyle.

**5 What was the outcome? What happened?**
I felt supported, confident, listened to and treated as an adult who might know something about her own body. I was asked to make another appointment in a month's time to see how I was getting on. The manner of the herbalist and his willingness to listen and answer my questions put my mind at rest and just generally made me feel confident and respected as a person.

## Negative critical incident

**1 What was the situation? What events led up to it?**
I had a suspected urinary infection. I had it a week and it wasn't getting better. I went to the clinic to make an appointment – the receptionist kept me standing there whilst she finished on

the computer. She didn't smile at any point. She saw there was a cancellation later that morning and I said I could come back. I came back ten minutes late (my watch had stopped). She said she would tell the doctor I was there and I should sit down. I sat in the waiting room for thirty minutes. Two other patients went in to see my doctor. I went back to the receptionist (long queue, only one receptionist for eight doctors, other staff in the back office chatting) and explained I was still waiting and I had to go soon. She rang the doctor who agreed to see me next.

## 2 Who was involved
The receptionist, the doctor and me.

## 3 What did you think, feel or want to do in the situation?
I felt unwell and wanted kindness and understanding but I also wanted to get better.

## 4 What did you do, what happened?
When I saw the doctor, she started off by explaining that if I was late I could expect to be kept waiting; she couldn't make others late. I asked how long I might have sat there and she said until someone else was late. She was assertive, unsympathetic and clear that I had no reason to be annoyed (not unreasonable, I had been late, but not very customer-focused). I explained my complaint, provided a urine sample; she said it looked as if it was an infection, said they didn't now send samples away to be tested and gave me antibiotics. I asked if she could take a swab too, relative to the comments in my notes regarding an earlier problem. She agreed. She said I could phone in for the results and another prescription would be left for me if necessary.

## 5 What was the outcome? What happened?
I felt like a number. I felt annoyed. I didn't entirely have confidence in the outcome and was glad it was nothing serious. I felt glad I knew enough to ask for a swab. I feel this patronizing "you're lucky to be here at all," unfriendly, disempowering style of medicine is unnecessary and pretty appalling. The clinic had a poor reputation in my area but they are fifty yards away from me. Nevertheless, I feel I will change doctors.

*Noting the behavior cues*

### Extraversion (E):

(i)   The medical herbalist allowed Mary to talk things out.

(ii)  Mary responded promptly to both the receptionist and the doctor.

### Intuition and Feeling (NF):

(i)   When she saw the herbalist, Mary enjoyed the interest taken in her. On the other hand she resented the doctor who made her feel like a "number."

(ii)  Mary showed interest in alternative therapy and appreciated the wider advice in terms of lifestyle.

(iii) Mary expressed pleasure in being listened to and reacted against the doctor who did not take time and show interest in her personally.

### Judging (J):

(i)   Mary was fairly precise about the time involved in the second example and explained the reason for her late attendance. She was also very conscious of her lateness and of the waiting time at the doctor's.

(ii)  She noted that she had a follow-up appointment at the herbalist and this seemed to add to her satisfaction. On the other hand in the negative situation the focus on outcome and next steps was less clear – Mary having to ask for procedures.


## INTUITION AND THINKING

## ENTP professional: Jo, surgical nurse

In the ensuing case study look for the following evidence of the professional's preferences:

### Extraversion (E):

(i)   Preference for talking things out

(ii)  Speaking before thinking through the impact

### Intuition and Thinking (NT):

(i)   Focus on perceived intelligence and competence

(ii)  Explaining logical options

(iii) Professional rather than personal relationship

(iv)  Importance of honesty

(v)   Irritated by illogical behaviors

**Perceiving (P):**
(i) Interested in exploring and finding needs in the moment

---

### Positive critical incident

**1 What was the situation? What events led up to it?**
A patient was admitted for an operation. He was a writer and came in with some work to do while he was an in-patient. I found him very interesting to talk to, bright and intelligent. Some of the nurses did not like him because they thought he wasn't friendly. One night, some time after his operation, I went in to talk to him, he looked very down and said he wasn't good company.

**2 Who was involved?**
Me, the patient.

**3 What did you think, feel or want to do in the situation?**
I was concerned and wondered what was wrong.

**4 What did you actually do or say?**
He told me that the doctor had been in to see him. He had told the doctor that he was still having problems – he had had a prostate operation – with his waterworks. The doctor had just said it would take time. I sat down and told him what we normally expected in cases like his and what he could do to help himself. I found it easy because he was able to follow what I said and he made some notes as we went along. After a while, he said that what really worried him was whether he would ever have a normal sex life again. I felt it was important to be honest and so I said that I wasn't an expert in this matter but would make sure he did see someone who would be fully qualified to answer his question. I told him I was glad he had told me about it. I didn't sympathize because I didn't think he'd want that.

**5 What was the outcome? What happened?**
He was a patient with whom I had a good professional relationship, he trusted me and I respected him. After he left he sent me a card saying how much I had helped, it said it had

always brightened his day when I appeared to say, "Good Morning, Good Evening or even Good Heavens!" I liked his humor. I still have the card, it reminds me of a job well done.

## Negative critical incident

**1 What was the situation? What events led up to it?**
I was looking after a man who had had abdominal surgery. Due to complications, he was in hospital for a long time. He was not very bright and often ate things that were bad for him and was ill afterwards. One day, after a period of time in which he had been quite ill, I found him eating something that I knew and he knew he shouldn't.

**2 Who was involved?**
Me and the patient, other patients were listening.

**3 What did you think, feel or want to do in the situation?**
I felt annoyed, we had just got him better and kept trying to make sure he ate sensibly and understood why. I wanted to stop him being so foolish and making himself ill.

**4 What did you actually do or say?**
As I walked by his bed, I asked him what he was eating and he told me. I said, "Why don't you have two helpings?" and he replied "There's no need to be so sarcastic, nurse." The other patients laughed.

**5 What was the outcome? What happened?**
I felt annoyed with myself and sorry that I had shown him up in front of other patients. On the other hand, I really wanted him to use some logic and common sense in future. This incident did not seem to teach him anything, he went on the same way.

*Noting the behavior cues*

**Extraversion (E):**
(i) Jo describes herself as going to talk to the patient in the first story and successfully works through his problem in a "Talk it Out" mode
(ii) In the second story, she quickly regrets her comments about the second helping.

**Intuition and Thinking (NT):**
(i) In both incidents the intelligence level of the patient appears to be an issue for Jo, she seems to prefer the one whom she considers bright.
(ii) In the first incident she describes the usual progress for someone in this situation. When given further information she is happy to recommend someone else, since she is not "expert." In the second case she is very clear about the logical options although unable to convince her patient.
(iii) In the first incident she describes her relationship with the patient as being professional.
(iv) She states the importance of giving honest information in a sensitive situation and is then more immediately honest than she might wish in the second case!
(v) Illogical behavior – "eating things he shouldn't" – produces irritation.

**Perceiving (P):**
(i) In the positive incident, Jo allows the conversation to run on until it reaches a natural conclusion.

## INTP patient: Mark, lawyer

In the ensuing case study look for evidence of the following:

**Introversion (I):**
(i) Preference for thinking things through

**Intuition and Thinking (NT):**
(i) Logical options
(ii) Need for competency in the practitioner
(iii) Wish to be treated as intelligent
(iv) Importance of "knowing why"

**Perceiving (P):**
(i) Focus on process (*how* things are handled) versus focus on
    outcome (*what* is the result)

---

### Positive critical incident

**1 What was the situation? What events led up to it?**
Consult with a thoracic surgeon prior to a deep tissue lung
biopsy in connection with early diagnosis and staging of
Hodgkin's lymphoma. Scans had identified what appeared to
be a lymphoma node in my right lung, in addition to the previously diagnosed involvement of lymph nodes in my left neck.
This lung procedure was to physically inspect and likely
remove the affected lung tissue.

**2 Who was involved?**
Just the surgeon and I.

**3 What did you think, feel or want to do in the situation?**
I was upset and apprehensive . . . not so much just because
of the procedure although no one wants to have surgeons
mucking about in their chest, but also because of the events
that had preceded it. For nearly two months, I had been
dealing with a lymphoma diagnosis, although all tests had
indicated it was limited to my neck and could be treated with
radiation. Now I was faced with the possibility that my lung
was involved, and that the lymphoma was bilateral . . .
requiring chemotherapy.

**4 What did you actually do or say?**
He very clearly explained what was involved in the procedure
. . . using an anatomical model . . . explaining that they were
now able to carry out this procedure using small incisions
between the ribs and inserting optical fiber and surgical instruments in that way. He showed me a small piece of the optical
fiber. He explained the purpose of each incision (one for fiber,
one for surgical instruments, one for drainage) . . . how long
the procedure would take, how long for recovery, etc. He
noted that a few years prior, this would have required full

thoracic opening, i.e. spreading the ribs, so by comparison this seemed almost trivial.

### 5 What was the outcome? What happened?
I left feeling completely at ease and looking forward to getting the procedure over with. Two days after the surgery I was at home and painting a fence. His open and clear explanation enabled me to "own" what was happening and greatly diminished my apprehension. I have a strong need to understand why something is being done because the strength to deal with it comes from within not from strangers.

## Negative critical incident

### 1 What was the situation? What events led up to it?
I was a teenager . . . probably fifteen . . . going to the dentist.

### 2 Who was involved?
The dentist, his assistant, and me.

### 3 What did you think, feel or want to do in the situation?
Didn't think much about it, no one likes going to the dentist, but I had dental work that needed to be done.

### 4 What did you actually do or say?
I didn't really say anything. The dentist barely acknowledged that I was sitting in the chair . . . seemed upset or distracted . . . and launched right into the drilling etc. without saying anything more than "Hmm . . . let's see what we have here." At one point something happened and he and the assistant, both peering down into my mouth, said "Uh oh . . ." and then kept on working without telling me what was happening. My anxiety went through the roof. I can still remember it clearly.

### 5 What was the outcome?
I have had a great fear of dentists ever since, almost to the point where I cannot go to the dentist unless I am in great pain. Lack

of any information . . . and treating me as if I was not even there, much less human . . . made this an extremely unpleasant experience. I wish I knew how to find this person now so that I could tell him what an unprofessional and inhumane person he is. At the time, as a teenager, I didn't know what to say or do.

### *Noting the behavior cues*

**Introversion (I):**
(i)  Mark gives information about what he heard or experienced, not what he said. He records appreciation of the careful explanation but gives no sense of a dialogue having taken place.

**Intuition and Thinking (NT):**
(i)  In both incidents, there are examples of him looking at the options. In the first he describes his apprehension about the treatment as being logical because "no one wants to have surgeons mucking about in their chest." Later he records feeling better because the treatment is now better than it once was.
(ii)  The first incident provides information as to the competency of the doctor who provided the "open and clear" explanation. This was clearly not the case in the second incident where he remembers, long after the event, that he was handled incompetently.
(iii) Mark describes his need to understand what is happening, so that he can "own" it. He also indicates that by receiving full information he actually coped with the situation better than he might otherwise.
(iv) Knowing "why" is very important.

**Perceiving (P):**
How things were handled – for example, the process of getting an explanation or not – was the key.

### Summary

In this chapter, we have moved from introducing the theory of the MBTI to the practice. The critical incidents presented an opportunity for you to apply your learning as you looked for behavior cues. This will help you to gain more information from the next four chapters which involve specialist applications of the MBTI.

# 4 Using a knowledge of psychological type when breaking bad news

A difficult yet frequent aspect of health care is the need to break bad news. We want to bring our very best to these situations to help our patients and ourselves. As you may suspect from reading the preceding chapters, an individual's type preference makes a difference in what they find helpful and in what they might automatically offer to be helpful.

The purpose of this chapter is to examine ways in which a knowledge of psychological type theory might assist professionals when breaking bad news to patients and their families. It will develop the work covered in previous chapters and apply it to this key area.

When we think of breaking bad news we inevitably conjure up the kind of conversation where a doctor tells a patient that there is no further treatment available and that he or she is likely to die. Breaking bad news, however, covers a much wider arena than this, as our case histories will show.

The actual subject of breaking bad news can relate to apparently less serious and dramatic issues but these are areas which neverthe less will cause distress to the patient. It can involve anything from telling someone that that they will remain on medication for the rest of their life, that they need a minor operation, or even that their booking has had to be canceled.

Health care professionals, especially but not exclusively nurses, are also involved in "re-breaking bad news." Because they often have more prolonged contact with patients they may find themselves going over information which the patient has already received but is either checking out in some way or has repressed. It is a well-known fact that the more serious news often has to be repeated many times before it is heard, understood and accepted.

Having said that, the more acceptable the mode of communication to the patient, the more likely he or she is to take it in, as the following examples illustrate.

## A patient seeking information about a close relative

When I was in my early twenties, I accompanied my mother for her check-up with the cardiologist. She had cardiac problems but was fit and active, playing golf and keeping house. I am her only daughter and was planning to marry in two months' time and move a considerable distance from my parental home.

Having a nursing background, I wanted information about my mother's illness. What I really wanted to know was what care she might need in the future and how best I could help.

The doctor agreed to speak to me but unfortunately was busy and did not even offer me a chair. His response to my question about the likely future needs of my mother was:

> "The trouble with these people is they just drop dead one day."

The shock of such a direct response ensured that I was not only deeply upset, but also that I rejected the message totally. This was particularly unfortunate since the prediction came true within a matter of weeks. My mother did indeed die suddenly. I was completely unprepared.

The question I had asked the cardiologist had been a general one to which he had given a very specific response. Some years later, I discussed this with a colleague with similar type preferences to my own and I heard an approach to medical information that matched mine exactly. She spoke of her own illness and her need for information and ended:

> "I just want to know the general lie of the land."

Thinking back to that day, I could see for the first time that my very general question, asking for a picture of the future, could better have been met with words such as these:

> "If you are concerned about long-term nursing care, or a slow decline, both are unlikely."

> This response would have left an opening for me to ask
> further questions, if I wished.

It is clear from this account just how important it is for the professional to listen and observe the patient and match their style. The physician answered a "big picture" question (NF or NT) with "the facts" (ST) thereby failing to communicate and, at the same time, causing additional and unnecessary pain.

By contrast, the next case history illustrates a conversation that appears to have been positive, although the participants may have had contrasting preferences. It also demonstrates that a relatively positive outcome can be achieved even in the saddest circumstances.

## A palliative care nurse breaking bad news to a child

I was asked to visit a seven-year-old boy, who has a seventeen-year-old stepsister – his mother, a nurse, was dying of secondary bone cancer. As far as the little boy knew, she had a poorly leg. I was asked to prepare him for her imminent death. I visited him at home and sat in the lounge with him. His father, who was unable to speak to him about his mother's illness, was in the kitchen.

I didn't want to do it, I wanted her to have a 'poorly leg' too. On the other hand I wanted the child to know the truth so that he had an opportunity to use the time that was left and so it wasn't quite the dreadful shock it would have been if he didn't know about it at all.

I used a book that I know well and have used in similar circumstances. He read the story out loud. It is about a dog that dies – it is called "Forever in my Heart." As we went through the story, we talked about different aspects of death as they came up, like what happens to the body and what happens at funerals. At one point in the story, he said "I wish you had brought a different story."

When we reached the last page – which had an outline of a heart on it, there was a suggestion that the name of a special person who is going to die, or has died, could be written in there. He said he didn't want to do that and, again, he wished I had brought a different story.

I told him that I couldn't bring a different story because, like the dog, his mother wasn't going to get better even though the doctors had tried. I also explained that she wouldn't come home but that he could visit her and talk to her, that even if she was asleep she could hear him. Following my visit, he did go and visit and asked everyone to leave and held her hand, even though she was unconscious, and talked to her. After I told him I said that it must have been a big nasty shock and that he might not like me for telling him. He replied that it was a shock " but it was fair." This expression surprised and puzzled me.

As a result of this meeting, the father could speak to the boy about death. He joined us after we finished the book, having listened throughout. He confirmed that she was dying.

When she did die a few days later, the little boy was involved in arranging his mother's funeral.

This story illustrates both how difficult it can be to undertake such tasks and how vital it can be. The child moved from a position of apparent ignorance to one in which he could make a decision to speak with his mother and be better prepared to face her death. It also allowed his father to be more expressive once the truth was out in the open.

It also illustrates another point. The nurse concerned has preferences for Sensing and Feeling (SF). When she recounted the story she said that she had had to gather all her resources to remain truthful, even when she wished she need not be. The words "I wanted her to have a 'poorly leg' too" illustrate this beautifully. She used her less preferred Thinking function to come to the logical conclusion that the pain the child would experience served a very positive function in preparing him to cope better with an inevitably traumatic event.

This proved to be helpful in a way she did not anticipate in that the little boy was able to say farewell to his mother and take an active role in preparing for her funeral.

The nurse expressed surprise that the child said afterwards "but it was fair." The boy was, of course, demonstrating the Thinking function.

## Using an understanding of type when breaking bad news

A great deal of literature exists which provides help and support for those involved in breaking bad news. Some of it is quite prescriptive and involves terms such as "ground rules" (Buckman 1992) and "steps" (Buckman 1992, Kaye 1995) although there is acknowledgement of the important need to:

> tailor our information sharing with the patient.
>
> (Buckman 1992)

All agree that training in communication skills is essential and that:

> Breaking bad news is a skill that can be learned and can be used in a busy clinical practice.
>
> (Buckman 1992)

Despite this plethora of excellent literature, it is unfortunately a fact that in many cases "it continues to be badly done" (Franks 1997).

Franks expands this idea by pointing out that "talking and communicating with people are basic human skills" which involve "basic techniques." She adds that "blueprints" are not desirable since they cannot cater for all possibilities. While type may at first sight seem like yet another "blueprint" you will already have seen that it contains within it the possibility of responding to the behavior that is *currently demonstrated* rather than working to a preconceived plan. The important difference here, therefore, is in ensuring that health care workers take their cue from the patient, not a fixed model.

The other important difference when using type in communication is that the professional knows their own type preferences and the ways in which they typically respond. This self-awareness can help a great deal, particularly when communicating with a patient who shows very different preferences.

It seems important, therefore, that the available models are taken, as they were no doubt intended, as aids rather than crutches. Many existing models have great merits and can be used in conjunction with type theory.

An understanding of psychological type, as we have already discussed, can greatly improve the quality of communication between two people. The fact that breaking bad news is a particularly sensitive process makes the use of type even more important.

Just as type maps onto communication generally, so it does onto breaking bad news. We have previously worked with the FLEX Care model, breaking the interaction into four main phases:

- Initiating the interaction
- Investigating needs
- Suggesting a course of action
- Next steps and closing

Initiating the interaction will continue to be influenced primarily by preferences for either Introversion or Extraversion. In Chapter 7, we will address more fully the connection between expression of type and stress but it is important to note at this stage that patients may not act "in character." This provides an excellent example of the value of the FLEX Care approach, observing the current cues, even when we know the patient well. The usually talkative Extravert may be quiet and reflective, the quiet Introvert may deliver a stream of anxiety before sitting down.

A number of professionals who provided the data for this book spoke of "empathy." (David – see the case study on pp. 64–67.) One helpfully described as meaning:

> not putting myself in the patient's shoes – because I can't, it's obvious I haven't got their illness – but saying to the patient what I heard them say and the feeling it seemed to carry.

An example of this might be "you are telling me you have constant pain and you appear to be frightened by the intensity and concerned that it will never get better." In this case, rather than immediately "matching" the patient's behavior, it may be necessary to identify it, as illustrated in the previous example. Type language can help with this:

> You seem to need three things here, information about the cause of the pain, action to control it and an acceptance and under-standing of your fear.

While the same possibility holds true for each phase of the interaction, our data once again suggests that the most important way in which type influences communication is through the expression of the combined functions:

Sensing and Thinking    (ST)
Sensing and Feeling     (SF)
Intuition and Feeling   (NF)
Intuition and Thinking  (NT)

## Pilot study

In developing the FLEX Care model, not surprisingly the subject of "Breaking Bad News" was uppermost in our minds. At the earliest stage, a group of palliative care nurses were asked to complete a simple pilot questionnaire. This followed a spontaneous discussion between them about what they considered to be important when buying a car!

A group member with preferences for Sensing and Thinking (ST) began by saying it was important to read the brochures, check performance and compare prices. Another with preferences for Intuition and Thinking (NT) looked amazed:

> I just want a car and I want someone who knows their job to sell it to me. I usually know what I want instinctively (or I've researched it) before I arrive at the showroom.

Another participant with preferences for Intuition and Feeling (NF) joined in, saying that she took into account the whole experience. She commented that since she had a small child she could be sold anything on the grounds that it provided safety for her son. The color might also be important!

Those with Sensing and Feeling (SF) preferences in the group, like those with Sensing and Thinking (ST) preferences, were interested in having some car data but wanted to buy from a reliable source with good sales and after-sales service.

The important point here is that this group felt that they knew each other and type theory quite well but a whole new dimension emerged in this discussion. This information was then applied to their professional life with particular emphasis on breaking bad news. They were then asked to answer this question:

> How would you prefer to have bad news broken?

This was a small group, no more than thirty in total, but their responses fitted exactly with Brock's earlier findings.

### Sensing and Thinking (ST)

Those with a Sensing and Thinking (ST) preference, as we have already discovered, tend to prefer to hear "the facts." Those with this preference provided answers that were brief and concise, often set out as a list of words. Those appearing most often included:

Honest
Truthful
Open
Clear
Realistic

The clearest summary of the replies from this group was contained in the following answer, which is quoted in its entirety:

Honestly, openly, with explanations. Do not go round and round.

This section is brief simply because the answers were both similar and very short, which in itself reflects the findings for the ST preference found in other FLEX research.

### Sensing and Feeling (SF)

Those with the pairing of Sensing and Feeling (SF) have already been described as valuing service to others, for whom the creation of an accepting atmosphere is important. This was described by the pilot group very clearly when they spoke of "needing someone who was sympathetic," the majority using the words "kind and gentle." Others added:

I would like someone to soften the blow.
In a language I could understand.
Counsel and support available.

Many spoke of needing the support of relatives and friends.

This group, like the one previously described, tended to use single words but with a very different flavor. The responses reflected the value placed on the personal caring approach valued by SFs.

### Intuition and Feeling (NF)

Those with NF preferences are said to need support for their vision in terms of possibilities, honesty and a respect for their individuality.

Each respondent wrote a mini-essay. In the one case where a short phrase was provided, even that painted a picture in words:

> quietly, sitting down, with concern ...

This was followed by:

> how long have I got, don't want details i.e. symptoms or what is likely to happen, don't want details of treatment.

This describes clearly the need for the "big picture" of those with this NF preference, prior to considering their next move.

Another reported that she would need time to "throw the thoughts around my head" and would need to know "where now, even if the 'where now' was no treatment." Similarly:

> I'd need time to make sense of my feelings ... I would then get on living my life as fully as I can ...

> I'd need time for it to sink in, I'd be more distressed for relatives and would **hate** to see their pain ... I'd like to have **any** treatment if it meant a possible cure or prolongation of life.

Individuality was also mentioned·

> I would want to be treated as a PERSON ...

Each of these responses could be seen as highly individual and they certainly reflect clearly the descriptions formulated in the original work. The bold type, underlining and use of upper-case lettering reflect the precise appearance of the NFs' written answers. This in itself adds to the individualistic nature of their responses.

### Intuition and Thinking (NT)

Those with an Intuition and Thinking (NT) preference, as we have already discovered, tend to prefer logical options and require those with whom they interact to be competent and knowledgeable in the field. They also tend to focus on possibilities.

A number of respondents referred to a need to be told by a "professional" and all illustrated the need to address "logical options," as, for example:

I would like time to digest the word cancer and to think about implications for me and my family ... course of treatment if any, and options ... I would like the person to be honest and competent.

I would wish to ensure that the best possible treatment/care was provided.

What treatment/intervention will encompass in terms of Q of L and effects on prognosis, evidence of the above.

The last response was particularly striking and was provided by a cancer sufferer:

I would want someone to be honest and provide me with the information without my feeling they are making decisions for me ... that's frightening ... to me honest equals gentle and kind.

These replies illustrate the desire for honesty, control and competency which is a hallmark of those with a preference for Intuition and Thinking.

The last respondent appears to equate honest information with the quality of kindness. How different this interpretation of kindness is from someone with preferences for Sensing and Feeling, who asks for someone to "soften the blow."

The needs of those with NT preferences appear to be clearly set out by this group, being the only ones to adopt words like "competent" and "evidence" and express the desire for "logical options."

While this study was small and informal it provides a series of examples from which we can see the contrasting needs of patients, which are clearly reflected in the functional pairings. At the simplest level, it is clear that we have patients for whom information and competency are paramount and some for whom the driving need is a relationship in which they are seen as an individual.

## Follow-up study

A further study was undertaken to provide a greater breadth and depth of information. A similar question was asked of a much larger number of people from many different backgrounds both in the UK and US. The only requirement of respondents was that they knew their MBTI type preferences. The questionnaire used is reproduced in the Appendix. The responses very much reflected and amplified those of the pilot study.

This information is presented here in two parts; first an overview reports the needs of this group in overall communication with health care workers, followed by the more specific responses to the "bad news" question. These data illustrate the fact that, overall, the responses by type are consistent.

### Sensing and Thinking (ST)

In the second study, words and short pithy phrases consistent with previous data were recorded when respondents were asked what features were important in a medical visit or consultation. Some illuminating phrases were:

> Hard facts, a clear picture, allowed to make my own decision.
> The professional is thorough.
> Understanding what is wrong.
> Can get me an appointment with the best specialist if necessary.
> Ask questions, identify problem, and agree action to resolve.

In terms of breaking bad news:

> To hear it straight, what diagnosis is about, how to cure.
> An explanation, a prognosis.
> Honesty, sympathy (to an extent).
> Pulling out all the stops to make it right.
> Clarity and realism.

A number commented on the need not to be patronized, summed up by the short statement, "and not to call me dear."

It can be seen that the responses tend to be factual and impersonal and even when the issue of sympathy does arise it is placed alongside the caveat "to an extent." The clear message from these respondents is, as the literature and our experience suggest, those with preferences for Sensing and Thinking ask for a factual straightforward, step-by-step approach and to be treated with respect.

In a FLEXCare workshop, a group of Sensing/Thinking types were asked the same questions and confirmed that in this situation they would want the facts:

> with no fuzzy prelude.

When asked to explain about this they all agreed that a "fuzzy" prelude simply made them anxious that bad news was being covered up and that they were not being treated as adults. The Intuitive/Feeling types responded to this by recognizing that, for them, an introduction of a personalized nature was essential but that it clearly wasn't universally welcomed.

### Sensing and Feeling (SF)

The follow-up study provided more supporting evidence for the idea of needing a factual approach combined with a strong need for relationship for Sensing/Feeling types. When asked what was important during a consultation this group responded:

> To be listened to.
> To feel part of the direction taken.
> Friendly, sympathetic, able to listen, encourage me to ask questions.
> That they give me their full attention.
> Not to be hurried or rushed.
> Sympathetic approach.

When bad news is involved:

> To be told fully but in a kindly way.
> To be supportive, "I'm here if you need my help."
> Someone else with me.
> Empathy, personal attention and good timing.
> To be told gently and not bluntly.

The last phrase, when contrasted with the "hard facts" quoted in the Sensing/Thinking section as a possible requirement, provides a stark contrast between the potential extremes contained in the responses when analyzed into functional pairs.

In a FLEXCare workshop a group of people with preferences for Sensing and Feeling recorded similar needs: to be given factual information but delivered at a steady pace by someone with a gentle approach.

### Intuition and Feeling (NF)

These responses seem to reflect clearly the work of Pearman and Albritton (1997) when they refer to "unconventional thought processes." Brock's (1997) work, too, refers to the expressed need for personal recognition, the wish not to be given too many details and, almost as a summary, the phrases "Recognize me as a person" and "Make me feel like I'm special."

The follow-up study confirmed these findings in relation to preferred consultation styles:

> That I feel he/she generally cares.
> Value me.
> That he/she recognizes it is my body.
> That the doctor listens attentively to me in a non-judgmental friendly attitude.
> Treated as a whole person.

Asked about hearing bad news:

> No doom, I don't believe anyone can know.
> Respect for my personal autonomy.
> Prayer.
> To feel they will not give up on me.
> Time to think, not too much information.
> Show empathy.
> To be given the facts diplomatically.

As with the Sensing/Thinking type who asked for sympathy, but not too much, here we have an Intuitive/Feeling type unusually asking for facts, but adding the need for a softened approach, "diplomatically." This is in contrast to the Sensing/Thinking respondent who asked for "it straight."

### Intuition and Thinking (NT)

This group had the need to be seen as competent and not "spoken down" to as a priority. They ask for logical options to be delivered by a professional who is also competent.

The follow-up study drew the following responses in relation to consultation needs:

> That I am not patronized.
> Complete concentration from my doctor (i.e. not looking at a computer screen but me).
> Skilled, knowledgeable, proficient.
> Being treated as intelligent.

Confidence in their competence.
Involve me, respect my intelligence.

On the question of breaking bad news, the following responses were forthcoming from this group:

To be skilled, supportive and honest.
Realism, a sense of perspective, not patronizing.
Open practical discussion of treatment, options and prognosis.
Complete honesty about particular problem, what will happen next, what I should do meantime.
Honesty, genuine concern without sentimentality, open-minded approach, an understanding of my beliefs.

These responses, as stated in the introduction to this section, focus clearly on the need for both the professional to be competent and the patient to be deemed to be intelligent. Again, there is an example of a softer word, "concern," being somewhat mitigated by use of the qualifying "without sentimentality."

## Clinical application

In order to amplify the data we interviewed health care professionals working in the field of palliative care. The interviewees work together and at the time of the interviews were not familiar with the MBTI. We used a semi-structured approach to the discussion. The interviewees were asked to share their experiences of breaking bad news under three headings:

1   What strengths do you bring to breaking bad news?
2   What do you find more difficult or challenging?
3   What impact does being involved with this kind of communication on a regular basis have on you?

We found that approximately 80 per cent of interviewees who were currently involved in palliative clinical practice preferred Feeling. That figure reflected Allen's previous experience.

After the interviews the respondents took the Indicator and validated their MBTI preferences. The full MBTI type of each practitioner and a variety of types will be included in order to present the full picture. As you read each interview you might like to consider what behavior cues are being demonstrated.

*Sensing and Thinking*

## Joanne, ESTJ, senior nurse

I feel comfortable following it through, returning to it. It is uncomfortable with a family I don't know, on the other hand it can be difficult if you know people well, you feel you are letting them down, professionally you feel a moral obligation to be able to break bad news well – if not you are withholding choice and information.

It is not always as bad as you think, it can be a relief, depends how it is done, times and choices.

You need a good background knowledge. If you know them really well, maybe years, being able to show a degree of emotion. For them to see you as feeling sad or guilty is a good thing. If you don't know people, that's intrusive. If someone I didn't know was like this, I'd think they were unstable.

I always find a release mechanism at home, but recently my husband left me and I have reverted into my shell, I haven't given as much as I used to. My husband said it was partly because I gave all to my work and needed to talk when I got home, I was unaware of that.

## Vivien, ESTJ, nurse manager

What I give is my experience of life, I have had a number of bad events, I lost my own father, so I know. My experience has made me more mature. We had a patient whose daughter was a palliative nurse specialist and the staff found it difficult to relate to her, the daughter, they felt threatened by her position. I found a way to do that.

I know there is a space around some people because I have a space around me.

I have an awful personal fear of getting it wrong – in anything. Both for me and them. I remember mistakes, even minor.

When I get it right, it is great.

You sometimes feel you can't take another one, especially when it is happening at work and home. On the other hand I am glad they come and ask me, I feel good if I can help. I tend to take a deep breath and talk it over with someone else – or go to a church for bell ringing. Then I can forget.

## Sensing and Feeling

### Fiona, ISFJ nurse

I guess I give information and clarification – it can be shocking news or what they already know. I often have to tease out what patients are frightened of – death or how they might die.

My approach is sometimes overly sentimental and empathetic – I sense I can be overly sympathetic. Patients sometimes want to make *me* better and I have to remember to focus on them!

On the positive, a very sick patient, a ballerina who had been branded neurotic by a doctor, suffered the worst form of cancer for her (it was very disfiguring). I tried to enter into it with her and she recognized that, "I know you know," she said. She liked me to enter into it.

People who are intellectual and clever don't want sentimentality, the "Oh, poor you bit." For example, one patient, a priest, seemed quite cold and distant – didn't want to be breached. He wanted factual information, my inclination was to scoop him up.

I try to back off and be more distant, I limp off and think I didn't do it right. In life I don't relate well to those kind of people. I am not hugely scientific, it helps to be able to interpret tumor behavior – but I am more able to talk about dogs!

When things go wrong, it makes me miserable, sad and anxious. I expect disasters – I hit the gin. I take great comfort in nature, I walk the dog, ride a horse.

## Georgia, ESFP, nurse

A patient I had been involved with who had a brain tumor had wanted to see the New Year in. She died in November and I was riddled with guilt that she didn't make it. Next day, a patient said, "Where's Wendy?" I said, "She died last night." The patient flung his arms round me saying "Georgia, I can't take another death." I hugged him, he cried – I hate it when men cry and said "Neither can I."

I went to the doctor, he listened to me, I told him, "I can't lose sight of these people." He told me to go and do just what I wanted to do, no prescription, I was so grateful. I felt nothing, it was devastating.

It is terribly important that patients trust you, truth is vital. When there is no further treatment you have to trust your life experience. I communicate that whatever happens I will never give up on them – I can see life when other people have given up – I have a tremendous amount of energy that has to be used – I give patients energy. We can always do something, that's our job. Patients I find difficult are the takers, those wanting attention.

*Intuition and Feeling*

## Christine, INFP, doctor

I think most patients think I am telling the truth, they trust what I am saying. I am quite good at taking it in little steps, at their speed. For some patients I think I am quite good at helping them see something positive in it . . . in that there is something we can do – or a spiritual dimension. More often it is practical but it is more satisfying if they can see some side of the spiritual development. Some patients have a feeling I am on their wavelength and that may push the conversation in that direction – the spiritual dimension.

I am fairly flexible, it is mostly fairly intuitive – I only make plans about what I might say if it is someone I don't know or who may be difficult. My experience is that plans don't work!

I find big groups difficult, families. There is no focus, I never know who to look at – so much to be aware of – often there is aggravation and large groups often have different ideas, often that is why we have to see them together in the first place. Usually I feel a bit threatened, especially if someone is aggressive when I can't give the answers they need. They do make me feel quite angry when they appear to be pushing their concerns above the patient's.

I find it difficult to talk with patients from whom I get no feedback at all, they appear to hear but from behind a glass screen, somehow there is no communication.

I do not worry as long as I know I have done my best, it worries me to think I've not given my best, or avoided something – then I worry. I don't talk about my work a great deal, but it helps mulling things over with nurses on the ward.

### Elizabeth, ENFJ, senior nurse

I like to know the background about the patient, that helps enormously. I will vary my approach slightly, some patients are very open, very quickly and that's simple – I find being honest very much easier, so I like permission to be honest with them.

What I find difficult is when I don't get anything, "I don't care" kind of messages, I don't know what they are thinking or feeling, or if they are depressed I find it difficult to communicate with them. I feel shut out from that person and feel a nuisance to them. When you want to help you need to back off and that's hard. Sometimes you get used to talking on a certain level quite quickly and when it goes wrong it is quite a shock. Often when it does it is because I didn't have enough background. The last thing I want is to pull the rug from under their feet.

If I know time is short and they have things to do, they need an adequate insight into their prognosis to deal with unfinished business.

My qualities, I have a fairly quiet manner which people seem to like. I *really* do like people. If they are being difficult I really want to be their friend and get a smile, that makes my day. I never forget it is a privilege to be with people at this time when they need to share. I don't mind sharing a bit of me if that helps. I like to think I give them a little personal touch, I think treating them as an individual, all with very different needs.

When patients resist – it is hard, tempting to switch off from them, I do tend to give them that space but remain open in body language, but it's hard.

Mostly I can walk away, and switch off by the next day. My life is busy and my children help. I go out when I am upset. When I develop a special relationship with a patient, it does stay with me longer. I try and turn it into a positive experience. I find it helpful talking to my colleagues – but not straight away. I find it hardest with younger patients, with children the same age as mine.

## Intuition and Thinking

### Rachel, INTJ, nurse practitioner and lecturer

I think one thing I am reasonably good at is giving people the opportunity to consider what is being said. I am quite comfortable with silence, even protracted silence. Mostly I recognize when that silence is appropriate.

I am not good at giving bad news over the phone because I don't like it (for example, if someone has died). I dread it especially if I don't know how the people – if it is someone I know then I'm usually up-front because the reality is that I will have to use the framework I always use:

- Fire the warning shot
- Break the news
- Within a time constraint – I have a time limit within which I have to work

(At this point, Rachel used her hands – holding them straight up and rigid, palms facing but a few inches apart, to quite clearly define that boundary.)

This is a model I have learnt and it makes sense so I always use it, not just on the phone.

From experience, I know that pussy-footing about and not breaking the news cheats the person of some opportunity to explore anything they want to.

I actually quite like it (breaking bad news), in that there are lots of things that I can do that are helpful at the time, that not every professional would know or feel and so, in some ways, I see it as a privilege for me and a bonus for them – the patients and the families.

I undertake the task without being aware that I am doing so. If I think it is going to be hard for someone else, I consciously make the decision to do it. Actually because it is something I feel OK about doing, I may have the need to do it so it is done right . . . a need for control, perhaps.

I do get very tired.

## Helen, INTJ, senior nurse

My strengths, experience, especially with women and I am used to working with patients and families together and I am comfortable with that. I am fairly good at letting people run with what they want to discuss. A diagnosis may mean different things to different people. I am able to step back and have a wider picture and awareness of perspective. I am fairly logical, I like things to be fairly systematic – people need that when things are frightening. For example, a doctor on a round said to one patient, "You have liver cancer, I can't do anything more for you" and walked off. I left him to manage alone and went back and told the patient "He's wrong, you have got liver cancer, but there is plenty we can do for you." I then gave her a number of options. She said she didn't mind the cancer, she had been frightened that nothing would be done to help her.

Sometimes I want to be positive, when patients want me to be – it's a kind of nurturing thing, you want to make it better – but I know it wouldn't be appropriate, "Please would you collude with me in denial." I can't do that.

> Empathy is important, being able to perceive someone's feeling regarding their situation.
>
> I have to have a distance to protect myself, I am conscious of that.
>
> Impact, on a very individual basis – there's always a certain patient who gets under your skin a little bit – a bit of you goes with them, but you gain something. I feel pressure to reach the ideal. I am very self-critical. I expect very high standards of myself and am very self-critical.

## Focus on the Thinking and Feeling dimension

One thing that became clear in the interviews is the special difficulty that nurses with a preference for Feeling experience with patients in a Thinking mode. This reinforced the idea that this is a crucial dimension in terms of human relationships.

The Thinking mode patients in question were identified as possibly being intellectual, being distant or giving no personal responses. In Chapter 2, we outlined the advantages of flexing with the patient. In this intimate and complex form of communication this may well be difficult for these professionals who feel rejected and unable to use their primary skills.

To tease out the strands of this dilemma we must return to the word "preference." It is important not to forget that these patients, however cold and distant they seem, probably have a need to share their feelings but in their own time and in their own way. There is a risk that when these feelings are released they may be very powerful. We will explore the effects of stress in relation to different type preferences in Chapter 7. It is equally important to understand the frustration and pain experienced by the professional involved. To be unable to ease a difficult situation by using the empathy and caring that may come automatically and is often welcomed, seems tragic.

There are two possible solutions to this dilemma. First, where teams have an understanding of personality type theory, those members with a Thinking preference may be able to help with the patient in the Thinking mode. While it is important to recognize that everyone is an individual, it might be possible to identify common themes. The interviews suggested that the nurses concerned were aware of the perceived "barrier" and tried to respect it; it would be helpful for them to understand that the barrier might represent a type preference for

Thinking. Feeling types recognize a barrier when some people do not express the personal impact of the situation. They feel at a loss for what to do because the "impact on people" is such a strong value for them. Having the type framework helps to give perspective on patient interaction.

From the perspective of the patient in a Thinking mode, however, the need is to be valued for what they are. This creates a climate of mutual understanding for them. Once this happens they can begin to take in what is happening to them. If they sense that something is required of them that they cannot provide, they are likely to with-draw. If, on the other hand, their need for either "straight information" or "logical options" is honored, they may be able to move into a more personal relationship with the professional.

Another example of how to cope with a Thinking–Feeling differ-ence in practitioner and patient was provided by an interviewee, Sally, who was able to use her best skills authentically. She provides mas-sage and reflexology in addition to nursing care. She prefers Feeling (ENFJ) but understood that not all patients responded to an open shar-ing of values or personal issues. She talked about a patient who attended the day-care unit in order to have reflexology. While he was there, he had other treatments and talked with many people – other patients and staff – but he continued to be of the opinion that he came only for reflexology. Just before he died, Sally visited him at home to give him a reflexology treatment. He did not talk about his cancer or his personal reflections on his imminent death. Afterwards they walked down the garden, which was a huge effort for him. Sally said to him, "Fred, you have had a wonderful life" and he said, "I know." Sally had been able to honor Fred's needs, even though they were dif-ferent from her own.

She then described the fact that the very way in which she conducts massage sessions helps to release emotions for many.

> I start with the patient face down, I am anonymous. They just focus on touch and then relax – tends to restrict conversation to "Does this help?" and so on. Questions about the physical body, then I turn them over taking care not to uncover them, they are wrapped in towels. We then have verbal and facial contact, but also I go to the head and neck – this is when emotional contact takes place – the release – it opens up conversation about their worries, their illness and how they are going to cope with their emotions and those of others. Because I see them every week the level of sharing can get greater over time.

What Sally seems to achieve, with an unconscious skill, is allowing people, whether in a Thinking or Feeling mode, to express their emotions in their own time. At the same time, she is able to use physical touch appropriately to facilitate the process. It seems as though when the initial treatment is non-verbal it is possible to "get past" the logical barrier; it short-circuits the defences and then goes deeper and deeper, especially where the professional concerned presents as non-judgmental.

## Exercises

1   Reflect upon the situations in which you have been involved in breaking bad news. Think about situations that went well and those that did not go so well.
2   From those experiences, define the qualities you bring to patients in this setting. Similarly, identify any difficult areas. Finally, consider how being involved in this kind of exchange affects you personally.
3   Now look back at the case studies and list the cues that fit your own experience. To what extent can you link your strengths and difficulties to a particular type mode in both the patient and yourself.
4   Reflect on your strengths and the things that you might want to do differently.

## Summary

This chapter, and the examples provided by practitioners, underline both the challenge involved when breaking bad news and the importance attached to doing it as well as possible. It illustrates that an understanding of the type framework can help health care professionals with this responsibility. The examples demonstrate that often practitioners are already aware of the behavior cues and an understanding of type can help them to further understand what they already recognize. Completing the exercise will assist with identifying appropriate actions to take in future encounters.

# 5  Adherence – encouraging patients to follow clinical advice

We have now looked at the theoretical background to type and provided many examples of how it works in practice. Moving on to the subject of adherence (also known as compliance) we can connect several of these preceding threads together in this important area of communication.

In this chapter we will:

* Discuss the importance of adherence.
* Examine the factors influencing patient adherence.
* Consider how an understanding of type can help professionals provide information for their patients which will help them to reach an informed decision – one to which they are more likely to adhere.
* Provide examples of how professionals and patients with different type preferences prefer to give and receive this kind of information.

Chapter 8, "Creating committed action," then takes this understanding of how to flex to patient preferences one step further. It provides a roadmap for how to create the dialogue necessary for patients to take committed action.

## The importance of adherence

Where the advice provided by the health care professional is both informed and constructive, it is clearly in the patient's interests to cooperate. Yet we can all recall times when we did not want to follow guidance relating to our health, especially when it involved something we did not want to do.

There is evidence (Levinson and Rotter 1993) that overall patient adherence is low. This may well be related to the fact – evident both in medical literature and from our own experience – that many practicing health care professionals have not had training in basic communication techniques (Meichenbaum and Turk 1987). This goes back to an issue raised in Chapter 1, which refers to the past, when patients expected to be "told what to do" and doctors and nurses expected to be "obeyed" in a relatively non-critical way. It requires more communication skill to ensure committed action. An example of the cost of non-adherence is clearly illustrated by the fact that between one- and two-thirds of prescribed medications are either partially taken or not taken at all (Clark 1996).

Poor communication is costly on many fronts – wasted medication, continuous need for medical intervention when crucial advice is ignored, the costs of seeking second opinions, and hesitancy to use health care resources until an emergency exists. Importantly, patients may not achieve the fullest recovery and quality of life if they do not follow a reasonable regime.

As medical costs escalate, as issues of informed consent grow in importance, and as the frontiers of what is possible in medicine grow ever broader and more complex, the need for patients to be able to make informed choices grows greater. This means that the health professional's skill in all aspects of patient communication and consultation is even more crucial.

## Promoting adherence

Encouraging adherence is an activity in which health care professionals are most commonly involved as they encourage patients to pursue a certain course of action. Adherence ranges from simple straightforward advice to complete a course of antibiotic treatment, even when the symptoms have gone, to providing facts about a more complex and radical change of lifestyle such as may be necessary initially for a severe diabetic.

Many factors may affect the way in which the patient receives any new information. The severity of a condition and the likely prognosis might encourage those normally least likely to follow instructions to do so. For example, British comedian, Eric Morecambe, had a frenetic lifestyle – always striving for better presentation of his humor. When his heart began to fail, he was told he needed major surgery. An interviewer commented on his courage in going ahead with the operation. Eric replied, for once without humor, that when he had been told that the longest he could expect to live otherwise was three months he found it an easy decision to make. Previously all advice to slow down and spare himself had been disregarded. On the other hand, severity of a condition and the patient's emotional reaction to it may almost completely block the patient's ability to take in and remember information.

The age of a patient may well be a factor – young people often find it impossible to imagine reaching the age of 40. They therefore see no point in changing a habit that is likely to cause chronic damage in later life. An older person may see no reason to stop smoking, "I've been doing it for thirty years and I am as fit as anyone."

The extent and amount of deprivation contained in a course of treatment may also be a factor. Lifelong medication, or permanent loss of some favorite food or drink, may be hard to contemplate without very good reason.

Finally, a number of changes may be required at once. An elderly man, who was very fit, found himself in hospital after an emergency operation that resulted in the formation of a colostomy. In the space of one hour on his third post-operative day:

- A physiotherapist visited and provided carefully expressed advice about the need to breathe in a certain way, cough a certain way and take regular short walks.
- A stoma-care specialist came and demonstrated how the colostomy would need to be changed and cared for. At this stage, the patient did not even know what a colostomy was.
- A nurse came to instruct him about how much he could drink each hour.

Each professional appeared committed and caring but none seemed to realize the combined impact of so many changes. In a time of increased specialization and choice, it is easy to overload patients with instructions without noticing.

In summary, many things can affect the way in which patients receive information and advice. Health care issues tend to be emotive and this in itself may lower the patient's ability to make sound decisions. Therefore, it is even more important to match the information to the patient and their needs. In the examples that will follow, we will see that professionals with different type preferences have predictably different ideas as to the best way of doing that.

## Improving adherence – using the MBTI framework

We have already illustrated how type preference impacts upon communications of all kinds. In particular we have noted the importance of the functional pairs in promoting or damaging dialogue.

In preparing this chapter we interviewed a number of health care professionals and patients and asked the following questions. In the case of the professionals:

> When you need to encourage a patient to follow a certain course of action, particularly one to which they may be resistant, how do you approach them?

In the case of a patient:

> What is important for you when a health care professional is encouraging you to take a certain course of action, particularly if it is one you might prefer not to follow?

We found, once more, that it was the use of the functional pairs (Sensing and Thinking (ST), Sensing and Feeling (SF), Intuition and Feeling (NF) and Intuition and Thinking (NT)) that provided the clearest differences from both the professional and patient perspectives.

The Four-Part Framework and information set out in Table 2.3 (see p. 46) – "To do's for type modes in health care settings" – provide clear guidance for use in all practical influencing situations. In the examples given below, the professionals' and patients' responses to questions of how best to encourage action and adherence are grouped in type functional pairs. As you read, note both the behavior cues and the degree of matching. It is important to emphasize here that it is not the intention of FLEX Care to persuade patients to comply passively with what the professional thinks might be good for them. Constructive use of the type framework encourages professionals to communicate with patients in such a way as to promote an informed decision that the patient can own. A particularly good example of this working in practice was quoted in Chapter 3 (see p. 56), when Zoe and her husband spent a long time discussing her treatment options with a consultant:

> We made a clinical judgment for ourselves. He did not put pressure on us, which was right. He was supportive and just gave us the facts.

As someone with Sensing and Thinking preferences, and a preference for Introversion, Zoe had needed time to hear and consider all the "facts" before coming to a conclusion: one that she still feels was right three years later.

The following statements show that patients and professionals of each functional pair want, or want to provide, information which improves adherence. The behavior cues of the type mode for each functional pair are included along with suggestions for how to best communicate with a patient in that mode.

## Sensing and Thinking (ST)

---

**Professional:**
- I would give them the information, the advantages and disadvantages; I might say, "How would you feel in a few years' time if this came back?"
- I try and tell them it would be good for them.
- I would ensure that I give consistent advice.
- I point out the benefits of what would be good for them. If that doesn't work, sometimes I am brutally frank.

**Patient:**
- I just want the facts, as much information as I can take in.
- I want to make my own decision, so I need a factual approach.
- I don't want a lot of sentiment, or personal stuff.
- I want to know the pros and cons from someone who really knows what they are talking about.

---

### *Behavior cues*

- Need for factual information, "I just want the facts."
- No mention of need for relationship, no "personal stuff."
- Logical approach, "pros and cons," "advantages and disadvantages."
- Need for competence, "someone who really knows what they are talking about."

### *Matching between professional and patient*

- Emphasis on facts and information.
- Need for logical framework.
- Lack of softer "relationship" words, for example "our, listen, or together."

# Sensing and Feeling (SF)

---

**Professional:**
- I see it as a negotiating process; it would depend on the patient. I'd listen to what was important to them and try and match the information to that.
- I try to take a collaborative approach. I believe it is always easier to work *with* people. Getting people to do things is not my forte – I don't like to lay down the law.
- I recognize that you don't need to say anything clever, people want me to listen, It is very important to really listen.
- I would ask a diabetic, for example, "What is it about a certain kind of food you can't do without?"

**Patient:**
- I need to trust the person with the information, have confidence in them.
- I like to be channeled into the right solution.
- I have to exist as a person, if only at the time of the interaction.
- I want individual attention, full concentration. I don't want a whole lot of wild options and alternatives.

---

*Behavior cues*

- Need for personalized approach, "I need to exist as a person."
- Wish to work together, be guided, "I like to be channeled."
- Need for listening and concentration, "I'd listen" and " I want . . . full concentration."
- Not wishing to be given "a whole lot of wild options."

*Matching between professional and patient*

- Emphasis on negotiation, "working with" rather than "telling" or "being told."
- Importance of listening.
- Awareness of personal needs.
- Options and "clever" ideas not being considered of value.

## Intuition and Feeling (NF)

**Professional:**
- I would use an analogy. With pain control, for example, I might describe a situation where a car is stuck in the mud. It needs a push, but if you keep it running, you won't need to push so hard.
- I sometimes go for theory, if necessary, but that would not be my first choice. Making a relationship is an essential part of the process.
- For most people I would initially make sure they truly understood, look at why they might be reluctant, what kind of person they were.
- Look for other ways of achieving the same result.

**Patient:**
- I need to know that the person talking to me has my best interests at heart.
- I want to be confident it is the right treatment and to understand why it has been chosen.
- It is important that we discuss steps that will work in my life, to keep me on course, for example, "Why not take a flask of herbal tea with you when you travel."
- If it is something I might not want to do, I need someone to spend time with me talking over the options. There might be something else for me. I'll need follow-up appointments to see how things are working or need to be adjusted.

### Behavior cues

- Need for harmony, importance of understanding, "my best interests at heart."
- Need for theory rather than facts, "I sometimes go for theory."
- Focus on vision, best interests and possible alternative options, "look for other ways of achieving the same result."

*Matching between professional and patient*

- Emphasis on need for understanding, that "they truly understood" and the need to "understand why it has been chosen."
- Need to present and examine options.
- Need for harmonious person-centered relationship.

## Intuition and Thinking (NT)

**Professional:**
- Depends on what sort of person they are – with lots of people you can give a rationale.
- There are some people who don't want to know, and are not capable of knowing – so with them I use a manager's voice, and they comply because of the authority. Sometimes you have to be more personal.
- I am straight, show them the good and bad aspects. I set a goal and don't avoid the negatives (if you do they'll find out anyway).
- I support people, recognize their difficulties – I can support lapses (when someone is supposed to be losing weight, for example) but there's always a cut-off line.

**Patient:**
- I need to know the reason for the treatment, the full extent of its effect: bad and good. I don't act out of faith in this regard.
- I want someone I respect to give me the information, not necessarily all the details. This gives me the inner strength to persevere when the going gets rough.
- I want the truth, even if it's not pleasant.
- I need confidence in their competence. If I have it, I'll pretty well do what I'm told. They need to understand my motivation; that's an important part of competence.

*Behavior cues*

- Logical options, "a rationale."
- Focus on competence and honesty, "I need confidence in their competence" and "the good and bad aspects."

- Big picture, "information, not details."
- Need for relationship barely acknowledged, "sometimes you have to be personal."

### Matching between professional and patient

- Emphasis on logical approach, "depends who it is," "what might happen if I don't – is it going to be worth it?"
- Importance of the truth, "they'll find out anyway," "I want the truth, even if it's not pleasant."
- Testing for competence, "confidence in their competence," "some people are not capable of knowing."
- The big picture, "reasons rather than factual approach," "a rationale," "give me the information, not necessarily all the details."

These examples demonstrate that professionals and patients with similar type preferences might expect to be "talking the same language." In the next two chapters we will develop this theme further. We will examine ways in which people of different and similar types might interact in team settings, and also our individual capacity to develop our less preferred functions. Returning to this context, however, it is quite likely that there will be a reasonable meeting of minds between those of similar preferences. The major problems are likely to occur between people with opposite preferences, ST and NF, and SF and NT.

Looking first at ST and NF and referring to the examples above we can see some possibilities for miscommunication. If the patient (NF) who stressed the need for someone with "my best interests at heart," or the one asking for time to talk over options, was consulting with someone (ST) who wanted "to tell them what's good for them" or be "brutally frank" it is easy to see where this might lead. Equally if a patient (ST) who requires "the facts" and "no personal stuff" is seen by a professional (NF) who talks about cars being stuck in the mud or who finds "making a relationship . . . essential" we can imagine the potential difficulties.

A doctor, with INFP preferences, recognized this latter problem from her experience with a patient in ST mode:

> A patient, when I was explaining why we needed to do something, just said, "I don't want to know all that, just tell me what to do."

A patient with preferences for SF needing to "be channeled" and "to exist as a person" might have difficulty with a professional with NT preferences who is "straight" and provides the options with a "manager's voice." From the other perspective, a patient with NT preferences, expecting "the truth" and obvious "competence" might be frustrated by an SF approach based on a personal perspective which excluded the need for unique ideas or "cleverness."

A patient with ISFJ preferences had difficulty with a nurse specialist in NT mode:

> She gave me so many optional treatments and then told me what the leading hospitals were using now. She seemed more interested in the current research than in me.

We can see, therefore, that when encouraging patients to comply with any regime, be it a diet or a course of medication, they are more likely to respond positively if they receive the information in a type mode which reflects their own.

## Exercises

1  Consider your own type preferences and reflect on your style of communication when trying to persuade a patient to follow a course of action.
2  Think of a patient with whom you interact easily. Identify which behavior cues match yours.
3  Think of a patient with whom you do not interact easily. Identify the behavior cues which do not match yours.
4  How could you modify your approach? Use the checklist from Table 2.3 ("To do's for type modes in health care settings") from the FLEX Care framework and list two things you could do differently.

## Summary

In this chapter, we have discussed the importance of adherence in a health care setting. We have identified a number of reasons for potential non-adherence, including type. We have provided examples taken from people with similar type preferences and found matching behavior cues. We have also viewed the examples from the opposite perspective, those with different preferences. It appears that the FLEX Care framework has potential for improving communication between patients and professionals, which could in turn improve levels of adherence. A roadmap for creating committed action is outlined in Chapter 8.

# 6 Working together

We have now looked at a number of applications of personality type theory. The emphasis so far has been on individual practice. This chapter will focus on how knowledge of the type framework can enhance the process of working together. We will look at:

- How type can improve team dynamics
- The role of written communication in teamwork
- The impact of change on teams and organizations

Each of these topics is extremely wide, whole books have been written on each one. We have, therefore, restricted the focus to type-related issues and used other models only where they serve to enhance understanding of type differences.

There are many ways of understanding effective teamwork. An understanding of type allows the practitioner to account for some of the varied reactions in a team setting. Active use of type differences in a team can help team members to value and incorporate alternative views and procedures more easily. In this chapter, the basic aspects of working as a team will be cited and the impact of type will be explored. Several examples will be given to show how team composition can affect a health care team's interaction. Finally, the ethical uses of type in a team setting will be discussed.

In this chapter we use the term "team" to mean both an interdependent group of people who can and must use each others' knowledge, skills, insights, and background to accomplish an identified task, and a more informal definition of team, that is, a group of individuals working together.

## TEAMWORK

Working together in teams has many advantages and can be very rewarding:

> When you ask people what it is like being part of a great team, what is most striking is the meaningfulness of the experience. People talk about being part of something larger than themselves, of being connected, of being generative. It becomes quite clear that, for many, their experiences as part of truly great teams stand out as singular periods of life lived to the fullest.
>
> (Senge 1990)

The phrase, "being part of something larger than themselves," reminds us of the phrase "the whole is greater than the sum of the parts." Energy generated by committed group action can be tremendous. An understanding of type theory can increase our confidence in what we have to offer and open our ears to what others offer.

However, for many individuals teamworking is not only unproductive, it is a kind of nightmare. Unhappiness between co-workers is very common and many training organizations will survive well into the next millennium because of the prevalence of non-functioning teams. Training alone rarely produces the answers:

> . . . managers by the thousands march off to all kinds of workshops and seminars, year after year, and more often than not come back excited and enthused about new idioms and approaches to supervision, only to return to their old ways a few weeks or months later. Charm schools and attempts to modify behavior seldom work.
>
> (Isachsen and Berens 1988)

Teams that do not function well are both costly and unproductive. The cost is often personal as well as financial; sickness rates can rise, and work time can be consumed by factional conversations. This is a particular problem in health care where so much personal emotional energy can be required.

The following aspects of team dynamics show in practical ways that an understanding of type mode can be used to enhance teamwork.

## Getting started

Getting started or forming can be approached very differently by different types. Team members with a preference for Sensing want to have a practical reason for coming together. Intuitives want to make sure the work of the team fits into the larger work of the organization or setting. Those with a Thinking preference want to get down to business – assess the goals, figure out what needs to be done by whom, set logical meeting plans and ways to evaluate results. Those with a Feeling preference want to spend time establishing personal working relationships. Who are we? What do we bring to this team? What do we personally want from the interaction? Is there a sense of caring about each other? In reality most people want all of the above, but it is the emphasis, amount of time, and order in which these issues are handled that can baffle team members if they are unaware of type preference.

## Structure

Structure and the need for it are seen differently by different types. Those with a preference for Judging report a sense of discomfort until a known structure is in place. Individuals with a preference for Thinking and Judging will generally want to structure the task. What do we need to get done? Individuals with a preference for Feeling and Judging will be more interested in structuring the relationships. Who will be doing what? How will we support each other? For people with a Judging preference, time is a valuable resource to be spent wisely. Structuring the situation cuts down on "wasted time."

Those with a preference for Perceiving are less interested in structuring the task to achieve an end point but are interested in how information will be gathered. They often prefer the freedom to use a wide variety of methods, including those that simply "pop up" along the way. Too much structure along the way feels cumbersome and will simply be circumvented or ignored. The individual with a Perceiving preference might say "Let's agree on the end point or outcome we're looking for, then be open to what occurs as we move forward." Measurement of team task effectiveness will be judged differently. Those with a preference for Judging will look at progress based on deadlines met. Those with a preference for Perceiving will be more likely to be concerned with the number of options generated (especially in the case of Intuitive Perceiving preferences) or the fact that a workable solution was found and we can quickly move on (especially those with Sensing Perceiving preferences).

Different tasks and situations actually call for different structures. An understanding of one's own type preference can build an appreciation of others' methods as well as help one move into other type modes when appropriate.

## Planning

Planning is generally acknowledged by all types as useful. Sensing types will often use past experience as a basis for current plans. Their favored time-frame is from the relevant past to the near-term future. Citing specifics and real examples is seen as helpful. Intuitive types will often favor the longer-term future in their planning. The past, though relevant, is less interesting to them than how various options may play out in the future. One method that captures both those with a preference for Sensing and those with a preference for Intuition is to plan for a range of circumstances: start with a plan that predicts little change; also create supplementary plans that factor in potential major changes.

Those with a preference for Extraversion tend to do their planning, when possible, with the whole team or sub-teams. They will use face-to-face planning days or retreats. Plans may shift as the interaction shows a need. Those with a preference for Introversion tend to do their planning quietly, often alone or with one or two people. They may put out a "white paper" for others to think about before an actual meeting is held. Without an understanding of type differences, it is easy to see that differences in planning style could be misinterpreted or that a single preferred style may be used even when inappropriate to the situation.

## Communication

Communication in a team is of course a central issue. How communication occurs is often a product of type preference without team members being aware of it. The amount of communication thought appropriate varies most directly with a preference for Extraversion or Introversion. It will come as no surprise that Extraverts prefer more interaction, especially in person or by voice-to-voice communication. These "talk it outers" literally experience more clarity, more ideas, and certainly more energy as they interact with others. Agendas may shift as the interaction takes place because new issues or insights are uncovered in the process. Those with a preference for Introversion often prefer quiet time to consider an issue fully before talking about it with others. These "think it throughers" appreciate an agenda and will generally read and think about it beforehand, if given an appropriate amount of time to actually do so. The trick here is to recognize that different types actually "do their best" under different communication conditions.

How things are expressed is also related to type. Those with a preference for Sensing use language that is down-to-earth, factual and specific. Expressing thoughts in conventional words that can be readily understood is desirable. They will often start with examples and move to larger principles – the inductive method. Their focus is on "what is sensible and realistic to do now." Those with a preference for Intuition use language that is metaphorical and prize unconventional or unique ways of expressing ideas. They will start with a concept and then move to the specifics – the deductive method. Their focus is on possibilities.

Often, Thinking types will analyze and use an "if this, then that" pattern as they communicate. They may sound critical as they analyze a situation, starting with what they see as not working. Even when giving praise they often add a "you might also try to," which is perceived by some as taking away the appreciation although the suggestion was meant to be helpful.

The topic of the communication often has a type twist as well. Those with a preference for Thinking will focus on the task. Those with Feeling preferences will often start the conversation with a note of appreciation, even when they need and intend to deliver criticism. Those with Feeling preferences will also include more personal pronouns, for example "our clinic" versus "this clinic." Feeling types use softeners in the delivery of their message, such as, "it may tend to work better if. . . ." Those with a Thinking preference will avoid softeners, appearing to be blunt. They might say, "it will work better if. . . ."

Communication about project completion varies with preference for Judging and Perceiving. Those with a Judging preference will say "We're on schedule" when all the pre-set checkpoints have been met on time with no last-minute fuss. However they will *feel* "We're on schedule" when pre-set checkpoints are being met ahead of schedule. For those with a Perceiving preference, "We're on schedule" is likely to mean "We'll have the outcome done and done well when it is needed," and not necessarily that the pre-set checkpoints have been met. For some Perceiving types, a last-minute push actually enhances the quality of their work.

# Meetings

Meetings are a fact of life for teams. Given the foregoing discussion it is probably obvious that type preference plays an important part in how meetings are used, structured, and held. Generally, those with a preference for Extraversion will view meetings as more valuable in the moment than those preferring Introversion. Meetings provide a "talk it out" forum which those with an Extraversion preference use to better form ideas. Those preferring Introversion often like some quiet thinking time in the meeting or after. It is actually beneficial for all to structure both "jotting time" and "talking time" into a meeting, especially if the issues are new or complex. If important decisions are to be made, a two-session structure may work well. The first session can be used to introduce and discuss and the next session can be used to consider other issues upon reflection and then decide.

# Conflict

Conflict, it is safe to say, is generally uncomfortable for everyone to some degree. Those with a preference for Thinking are often focused on the task of a team and so may be slower to respond to conflict as something to examine or resolve. However, once they have identified conflict as an issue, they are likely to move into a straightforward problem-solving mode. They want to find a logical solution then move on with the task in hand. Those with a preference for Feeling are more likely to be aware of conflict and want to resolve it. Because their focus is on people-oriented values, disharmony in the interaction is noted early. Their mode is often to find common ground or to surface the team interaction issues.

Successful teams must work effectively with both the task and relationship issues of teamwork. Obviously valuing the input from both the Thinking and Feeling modes allows the team to function more fully.

# Closure

Closure is often seen by Judging and Perceiving types in very different ways. As the team's successful work draws to a close, those with a Judging preference usually feel great. "Joy of Closure" is not too strong a label for the reaction of those who prefer Judging. On the other hand, as the project ends, Perceiving types often feel let down or do not feel much of anything. Their "Joy of Processing" has come to an end, at least until the next project. Celebration seems appropriate at the conclusion of a project for Judging types, while celebration at the beginning is more the Perceiving types' style.

## Ethics of teams

Using the MBTI in team situations can be very helpful, or very unhelpful. On the positive side, if used well it can break down barriers and encourage mutual exploration of individual and group strengths and potential weaknesses. Used inappropriately it can increase scape-goating and labeling. To illustrate this point, imagine there is one team member who tends to hold a minority view – one that is unpop-ular. When the MBTI is introduced he is found to be the only person with a preference for, say, Intuition. There can be a tendency for the others to say, "Well, of course his head is always in the clouds, I always knew it and here's proof." Type preference is not a label. It truly refers to preference only. All types can and do use all prefer-ences; they simply "prefer" some aspects over others when they can do what they prefer. The following section and Chapter 7 will address this issue in more depth.

## Appointing a team

Having read the preceding sections, it might be tempting to think, "Well, the thing to do here is just to select the right team members in the first place. What types do we need?" This, of course, is the wrong question; an individual's type preference neither assures nor negates ability. A team needs people with the skills necessary for the work. This means that the questions to ask are "What skills do we really need for this team?" and "How have these skills been demonstrated to date?" Selection simply on the basis of "difference" or on type preference will not produce the necessary result.

   An awareness of individual type preferences once a team has formed alerts members to ways in which the team may operate and what they may need to consciously develop. When members are all similar in type, they may experience complacency. This may lead to missed perspectives or blindspots. In a team where contrasts in type exist, there may be greater energy but conflict can result if that diversity is not used constructively. Both possibilities are illustrated in the following case study.

A group of three specialist nurses, supported by a secretary, provided community nursing care. The preferences within the team were as follows:

| | |
|---|---|
| Team leader | ISFJ |
| Nurse | ISFJ |
| Nurse | ISTJ |
| Secretary | ISFP |

The team provided a reliable service and the interaction between individuals was both supportive and positive. The leader was aware, however, that the team was going to have to increase service greatly due to an expanding demand. At this stage, she was unaware of the MBTI. She decided that the team needed people with different backgrounds and experience, but did not specifically define the necessary skills. Three new posts were advertised and the three candidates appointed had the following type preferences:

| | |
|---|---|
| Nurse | ESTJ |
| Nurse | ENTP |
| Nurse | ENFP |

The new "team" in fact never became a team at all. The new recruits' extraverted "talk it out" energy overwhelmed the existing members. Given the team dynamic a split developed. The original group clung to their previous existence. Among the new recruits there was a focus on new options (N) versus prizing what worked well and needed to be conserved. There was also a shift to task first (T) versus building relationships to accomplish the task (F). The new members became totally disillusioned. Despite intervention from a consultant, the team lost two of the new members within a short period. This pattern has repeated itself in different forms since.

What this case demonstrates is the potential pitfalls of unrecognized team dynamics. Type similarities and differences in a team *will* exist. The point is to use type as a way to understand team dynamics and individual preferences. Type gives team members a vocabulary and framework with which to celebrate differences and enhance team effectiveness.

## The role of written communication in teamwork

Throughout this chapter, and indeed through the whole book, we have been working primarily in the area of the spoken word. We now turn to consider the impact of the written word and how type impacts on what we write and what we prefer to read. Written communication is, among other things, a central part of teamwork. In the age of technology, electronically propelled messages move with great speed across thousands of miles, adding to our opportunity for ever-wider communication. This book has been largely written using this electronic medium, by two authors living on separate continents – a possibility that was unthinkable a very short time ago. The phrase "information explosion" underlines the importance of good communication skills in many different areas.

When we have to write a message, we often have time and opportunity to reflect on it before it is dispatched. However, we do not always make good use of that opportunity and, of course, in a busy world we do not always have it. Using computers and e-mail tends to increase speed and reduce time for deliberations to take place.

The potential problem with the written word is threefold. First, what is written can be interpreted in ways that we did not intend. Second, we may not know very much about the recipient and do not have the advantages of face-to-face contact, observing body language for example, as our message is delivered. Third, the receiver has "evidence" of the content and the writer is usually not present to explain any misunderstandings.

In summary, therefore, it appears that in written communication there is often a greater chance for us to think about the content in advance and "get it right." At the same time, however, we have all experienced times when it went seriously wrong.

> I had taken a new position as Training Officer in a small hospital. Soon after I arrived, I attended an introductory course on resuscitation. I learned a new method and was very excited by it. When I got back to work I sent a memo to the senior nurse in charge of the medical unit and explained that I had been to the course and was hoping he would attend the full course with me. He reported me to his manager saying that I was implying that he didn't know how to do his job.

This hurriedly composed but innocent message became entangled in something much more complex in that the nurse concerned felt criticized and threatened by the new arrival.

On the other hand, written communication which does "work" can be extremely rewarding. Most people keep some letters or reports that brought great happiness, often for many years. During that time they are re-read and enjoyed many times.

> I used to work for someone who always acknowledged the work I had done well, I passed my reports to her and they often came back with a note attached. She always commented in detail on my report and recommendations and drew out anything that she felt worthy of comment. I saved some of them, in fact I have still got some. I did a difficult job at that time and often worked alone, so it was very important to have this kind of feedback.

In this section we are going to consider to what extent type affects the way in which we write and the way in which we receive written communications. Clearly, in the examples above, there are more issues involved than type alone. In the first case, the senior nurse was resentful about money being spent on a training position, which he felt should have been used for extended clinical nurse hours.

There is, however, also a type issue involved. The training officer involved, who had attended the resuscitation course and was excited by the new ideas, had preferences for Intuition and Thinking. The account illustrates an apparently good idea which was not fully thought through from the "impact on people," Feeling, point of view. While an understanding of type may not have totally prevented this situation, it may well have helped.

## Using type to improve written communication

We may write to those we know and to those we do not. We may send a message to one person or a group of people. The one common denominator is us. Through an understanding of type, we can develop an understanding of our potential strengths and weaknesses in this medium and deliberately craft our written communication to appeal to the people for whom it is intended.

In order to do this we need to look again at the four dimensions of type. As you read through this section you might like to hypothesize about your own style of written communication and reflect on your own experiences. Think about your most important writing tasks – what type modes predominate in those who receive your written work?

### Talk it Out and Think it Through (Extravert and Introvert)

There is a general view that Extraverts tend to prefer oral communication while Introverts prefer to receive written information. This is true to an extent, since the Extravert, as we have already highlighted, often thinks aloud. Introverts, on the other hand, tend to find it easier to absorb and consider information in written form.

When it comes to written communication, Extraverts seem to plunge in as they do when speaking. Those who prefer to "Talk it Out" and have a "Joy of Processing" (Perceiving) use stream-of-consciousness writing that needs an edit for brevity or focus. Those whose "Talk it Out" preference is coupled with "Joy of Closure" (Judging) may write in summary form and with such definitive strength as to appear "done," even when reflection and additional input are desired.

Those with a preference for Introversion may well take more time to prepare a written message and may not be as openly expressive. However, just as we find that an Introvert can talk fluently on subjects in which they are knowledgeable and interested, they can also write at length when the situation requires them to do so. Those with preferences for Introversion can express their depth of interest in a subject, in this area, sometimes with more depth than the reader needs.

### Specifics and Big Picture (Sensing and Intuition)

People with a preference for Sensing, as we have already discussed, tend to use shorter, more conventional words. They may prefer to use short sentences or even bullet points in their written work. When writing, those preferring Sensing may be more down-to-earth in their approach, that is to say they are likely to concentrate on the practical issues of the communication.

People with a preference for Intuition, on the other hand, will tend to use longer and more conceptual words. Their messages are likely to sketch out the idea they are describing and the actual meaning may at times be somewhat obscure. Their written work may also go off at tangents. For example, a business letter written by someone with preferences for Intuition and Perceiving ended with the following paragraph which comments on the *process* of writing:

I was just checking this letter with the spell-checker. I had written a sentence which started "In a nutshell . . ." and it wanted to replace it with "In short." Can you imagine that? I pressed "Ignore"!

The other interesting aspect of this example is that the spell-checker appears to have suggested a replacement with a Sensing flavor!

In terms of overall visual presentation, Sensing types use bullet points and Intuitives often prefer paragraph format.

Those with a preference for Sensing may find communications from Intuitives complex and unfocused. A man with ISTJ preferences, who works with the MBTI, was reading a paper written by a colleague with ENTP preferences. In one rather complex area he wrote "You N's might understand this, but us S's don't!" Intuitives, in their turn, can find the writing of Sensing types to be lacking in imagination, as they see it.

### Logical Implications and Impact on People (Thinking and Feeling)

The Thinking and Feeling dimension is, once more, the area which can lead to personal misunderstandings. The approach taken by a Thinking type may be business-oriented or task-centered while those with preferences for Feeling may be more relationship-oriented and use a more personalized style.

People with a Thinking preference use a more non-personal and definitive style. As they might do in speaking, they may use the less personal third person, "*it will* be a better option for your unit." As this phrase illustrates, those with this preference may also avoid words that soften the edges of the communication. For example, they would not write, "my suggestion would be that you try a new option in your unit." They would find these "softeners" unnecessary and in the way when getting the task accomplished.

Those with Feeling preferences are more likely to devote time to personal inquiries before addressing the task objective. The focus here is relationship and process to help the task to go forward. This group is likely to use the second person and "softeners," "*you may* find this to be a better option for your staff."

Visually, written work composed by those with a Thinking preference often includes lists and a logical sequencing of information. They may also include an outline of a proposal or a flow-chart. People with a Feeling preference tend to include circular diagrams, and enjoy the use of color and mind-maps of ideas. This difference can be seen very clearly in Myers-Briggs workshops when Thinking and Feeling type groups separate to work with the same task. The group with a Thinking preference will present a sequential list of points, usually in one color, while the group with a preference for Feeling may well add colored illustrations to their answer. One group of Feeling types, for example, drew bunches of flowers and a heart next to the question, "How do you prefer to receive praise." Without an understanding of type, these groups inadvertently give their information in a format with which the opposite group may struggle.

The potential for misunderstandings and ill-feeling is encapsulated in the following examples:

> I work as a biochemist and have ISFJ preferences, my senior colleague has INTP preferences. I regularly receive notes in my in-tray that I find critical and hurtful. I experience this tone of writing hard, precise and angular. When I try to explain, he just says, "It was just an idea for you to consider."

This illustrates the potential difficulty with great clarity. The writer sees the message as conveying an idea, the receiver as a pure criticism because there is no personal recognition.

Looking at the same dimension from the other perspective:

> I work in human resources and have ENTJ preferences. I get reports from the senior nursing staff after they have conducted performance review interviews with their staff. I find some of them a bit short on relevant evidence, especially one from a manager with ESFJ preferences who always writes pages about the personal life of the nurse, most of which I find irrelevant. There is never any objective assessment of performance.

This example highlights the difference and potential for misunderstanding between the task-centered approach to performance review and the relationship-centered approach. As a reader, you may find your own preferences active while you consider these examples. Do you find one method more satisfactory than the other? Do you have a rationale for your judgment that "should" convince others? That is type preference in action!

## *Joy of Closure and Joy of Processing (Judging and Perceiving)*

A person with a preference for Judging, as explained earlier, has a tendency to use words which end with "ed," as, for example, "diagnosed," "organized" or "referred." Since they seek completion, their writing may reflect this and appear purposeful with no further input needed. The degree to which this may be apparent depends to some extent on other preferences. For example, someone with Sensing, Thinking, Judging (STJ) preferences may be much more direct and to the point than someone with Intuition, Feeling, Judging (NFJ) preferences.

Those with a Judging preference, as might be expected, choose ways to display tasks which structure and aid completion. Charts and task lists with date milestones to be filled in as they are completed are often used in project work.

People with preferences for Perceiving may have a more "exploratory" style and use words ending in "ing," as, for example, "researching," "discussing" or "prescribing." A more free-flowing style, often seeking further information or making new suggestions, may reflect a preference for Perceiving. In the same way as the Judging dimension, it is quite likely that Perceiving may show up more clearly when combined with Intuition (NP) rather than Sensing (SP).

Those with a preference for Perceiving choose ways to display data that leave room for spontaneous shifts and quick action. A simple list will often do. The list may include space for add-on notes.

In a health care setting requests for written communication often include a deadline by which it must be received. Because "by Wednesday" may mean "by the end of the working day" to a Perceiver and "8 a.m." to a Judging type it is imperative that any deadline be fully clarified.

## The functional pairs

In Chapter 2, we introduced the functional pairs (ST, SF, NF, NT) and we referred a great deal to their importance in communication. Phrases such as "different language" or "different dialects" have been used to describe the contrast between functional pairs.

Through collecting written data for this book, both from individuals' forms and from written report-backs in group settings, we have also been able to see the effects of type on written products. As we might expect, they reflect the patterns found in oral communication.

This information is presented in a checklist format to highlight what each functional pair prefers. Use this checklist when writing to those in different modes. Each functional pair list is followed by an example to visually illustrate differences. Written communication can be "tilted" toward the general patient population seen or it can deliberately include aspects that appeal to all types. Readers will generally skip over words and phrases that are less appealing and focus on the parts that are more appealing.

### Sensing and Thinking (ST)

* Short, to the point
* Precise qualifications if appropriate
* Bullet points
* Conventional words
* "Business-like" tone
* Factual

---

**ST**

**The Spenser Orthopedic Clinic, West Street, Bristol**
The Clinic provides a range of orthopedic services which include:

* Trauma
* Joint replacement surgery
* Sports injury service

All personnel are fully qualified and provide a first-class service at competitive rates.

Clinic hours:

9 a.m. – 1 p.m.
2 p.m. – 8 p.m.

Telephone number (24-hour service) . . .
Inquiries to the Clinic Director

---

*Sensing and Feeling (SF)*

• Short
• Bullet points
• Conventional words
• Personal tone, i.e. personal pronouns, specific quotes

---

**SF**

**The Spenser Orthopedic Clinic, West Street, Bristol (Established in 1972)**
We provide a full range of orthopedic services for our patients. We specialize in the following areas:

• Accident and emergency surgery
• General orthopedic work, including replacement surgery
• Personalized maintenance/injury regime for athletes

Our team aim is to provide an individual service to all patients. All staff are qualified and experienced. We welcome all inquiries from prospective patients.

Clinic hours:
9 a.m. – 1 p.m.
2 p.m. – 8 p.m.

Appointments can be made outside these hours by arrangement. Please contact the Clinic Administrator, Gale Peterson.

Telephone number . . .

### Intuition and Feeling (NF)

- Longer paragraph format
- Expressive, underlining, personalized anecdotes
- Unique words and phrases, personal pronouns

---

**NF**

**THE SPENSER ORTHOPEDIC CLINIC, WEST STREET, BRISTOL**
*"The Spenser Clinic is designed with your health in mind."*
Our staff are carefully selected from both traditional and non-traditional health care backgrounds, to provide a full range of treatments. We cater to all orthopedic needs from surgical intervention to the relief of everyday aches and pains. Your health comfort is our greatest concern.

Treatment is provided in restful surroundings. Our staff are available to provide the service you need. Clinic hours on weekdays are from 8 a.m.–6 p.m. Extended hours by arrangement.

We welcome informal visits and pre-treatment discussions. Patients tell us: "I didn't know such service existed today," "You cured my back and set me on the road to a healthier life," and "My time at the clinic restored not only my mobility but lifted my spirit."

If you would like to come and see us, please call Gale Peterson, our Clinic Administrator at . . .

**"WE LOOK FORWARD TO WELCOMING YOU!"**

*Intuition and Thinking (NT)*

- Longer, paragraph format
- Present the "why" or logic behind the idea
- "Business-like tone"
- Unique words/phrases, metaphors

---

**NT**

### THE SPENSER ORTHOPEDIC CLINIC
#### WEST STREET, BRISTOL

The award-winning Spenser Clinic offers a full range of orthopedic services provided by highly trained clinicians and surgeons. The clinic specializes in joint replacement surgery, using state-of-the-art techniques.

Our surgeons, therapists and caregivers, have been selected to work with athletes competing at the highest international level.

We provide a service that is unparalleled. If you need expert services, either preventative or curativo, contact our advice line . . . which is available 24 hours a day.

---

## Improving written communication

The information above highlights the fact that our written work can be considered in the light of the MBTI framework. Getting to understand the expression of our own preferences is relatively straightforward in this context. We need only review our own work critically. For example, someone with a preference for ENTP might need to check:

- Is the purpose of the message clearly stated? (the writing of NPs can appear obscure)

- Is the message too long, have overly complex words been used? (Ns tend to enjoy long words)
- In the case of a letter, is the stated intent of the letter too impersonal? (Ts can forget to acknowledge the other person)

The other potential source of help, when available, is to ask someone else to check the message. This is particularly helpful when the receiver has different type preferences from our own or when the message is highly significant, or of an especially sensitive nature or meant for a wide audience.

## Exercise

1   Write or choose a memo on a relevant topic and pass it to a colleague who you know often looks at things differently from you.
2   Ask what they would change to make the memo more effective for them.
3   Review the cues for type mode (see Table 3.1 p. 51) and consider whether your colleague's suggestions reflect his/her type mode.

## Summary

We have examined the links between written communication and the MBTI and highlighted potential strengths and pitfalls for different type preferences. The importance of getting written work to communicate well has been emphasized together with the understanding that more often than not we can take time to check this form of communication before sending it out.

## ORGANIZATIONAL CHARACTER AND PERSONALITY TYPE

Earlier in this chapter we looked at the importance of personality type in teams. We now intend to consider the implications of organizational character – what it is and the potential influence of type in organizations.

In health care terms, an organization might be a small autonomous clinic, an independently-based group of community workers or it might be a division of a wider unit, a hospital department, or a group of hospitals. All of these have a history and a character that are unique to them.

William Bridges describes "organizational character" as follows:

> An organization's character is like the grain in a piece of wood. There is no such thing as good or bad grain, but some kinds of grain can take great pressure, other kinds can withstand bending or shearing forces, and still others are lovely and take a fine polish. Some are too soft or hard, too light or heavy for a particular purpose, but each has some purpose for which it is well fitted.
>
> There are other metaphors: Character . . . is the personality of the individual organization; or it is the DNA of the organizational life form. The organization's character makes it feel and act like itself.

> (Bridges 1992)

How does an organizational character develop? There are a number of answers to this question:

- The character can depend on the function of the organization. To take a clear example, the character of a major banking company might well differ from that of a local co-operative offering debt counseling free of charge. In health care, a cardiac surgical unit might differ in character from a department that provides respite care for the frail elderly.
- The character is often established by the people who set up the organization. An example of this might be found in the non-profit sector, where an individual identifies a need for a service, and gathers a group of like-minded people together to raise funds and set it up. In health care, a group of professionals committed to a particular vision might collectively establish a new unit within their own specialty.
- The leader of an organization has a significant part to play in the character. Often when a leader is replaced a cultural shift takes place.
- This character is deepened over time by the type of people it employs and they in turn are attracted by the character and purpose of the organization.

Once a character is established there is often an unconscious pattern in which people with similar backgrounds gravitate to the organization, reinforcing the status quo. There is a tendency, as discussed in relation to teams, for individuals to offer employment to people "like me." "We share the same values and ideas, we can work well together." Therefore, the grain in the wood intensifies.

We might wonder whether, once a character is established within an organization, it could change. Bridges is cautious in his approach:

> Although changing an organization's character is certainly possible, it is difficult and takes more time and resources than organizations usually provide. That is why one finds that after all the big transformative changes have been made, the organization is still disappointingly unchanged in some very important ways.
>
> (Bridges 1992)

By comparing organizational character to the grain in a piece of wood, Bridges provides a clue to the connection between type and character. Just as type theory assumes no good and bad preferences, he explains that the grains are simply different and serve different purposes. It is important to remember, however, that those people contacting organizations as customers, inquirers or patients, may not share the type exhibited by the organization.

Bridges developed an "Organizational Character Index (OCI)" which was designed to explore how the MBTI preferences might relate to this wider field. The OCI is presented as a questionnaire in Bridges' book *The Character of Organizations*. Organizations can use this index in a way similar to that in which individuals learn about their type preferences using the Myers-Briggs Type Indicator. One important distinction between the OCI and the MBTI is that the OCI has not yet been substantiated in terms of its reliability and validity.

The following section applies some of Bridges ideas to the health care setting. In Chapter 1, you were invited to hypothesize your own type preferences. In the following section you might wish to carry out a similar exercise in relation to an organization for which you currently work or have worked in the past.

## Extraversion and Introversion

We first need to examine the source of an organization's energy. That is, where is "its reality" (Bridges 1992) situated, in the world of Extraversion or Introversion?

Extraverted organizations are, as we might expect, externally oriented. Typically, they tend to discuss ideas openly, make decisions quickly and keep abreast of life outside their own sphere of operations. In health care patient settings, this might be seen as encouraging relatives and friends to visit freely and to become actively involved in the life of the unit. In other areas the Extraversion may be expressed as a willingness to collaborate, to share ideas with others involved in similar work.

Introverted organizations are likely to be more internally focused. In health care patient settings, this might be seen in protecting the patients from too many visitors. In other areas, the Introversion may be expressed by a sense of privacy and reservation about sharing ideas with others, particularly if they are at an initial stage. Ideas may first be considered by individuals and then shared within the immediate group.

When difficulties are encountered, Bridges describes the Extraverted organization as generally setting out to find answers from outside itself while the Introverted organization tends to examine itself from the inside. As may be clear, either process, to the exclusion of the other, will produce less than optimal results.

Examples of health care organizations that we have found to have a preference for Extraversion contained within their character include:

- A residential care home for the elderly which holds lunches and coffee parties for non-residents. The owner leads a group of care home owners in the district and is in touch with local trends They are planning to set up a community service, with carers visiting people at home.
- A small local hospital which has an active fund-raising committee and is involved in community action on many levels. The hospital is often featured in the local newspaper for its outreach and is well known in the area.

Examples of health care organizations that we have found to have a preference for Introversion contained within their character include:

- A small day-care hospice, developed by a group of nuns and run within the convent grounds. Patients are referred from a group of local doctors but no community involvement is encouraged. The nuns were asked to consider a residential unit linked with the local hospital but felt it would stretch their resources to collaborate in this way.

• A specialist research unit, where long-term complex medical research is carried out. The employees are discouraged from discussing their work even with close colleagues.

## Sensing and Intuition

We now move to examine the ways in which different organizations take in information, what attracts their attention.

Sensing organizations tend to put their trust in traditional methods. They excel at handling large quantities of detail using set routines. Overall they prefer change that is incremental and purposeful, not "change for change's sake." Bridges describes Sensing organizations as emphasizing "targets and plans" while trusting "experience and authority."

Intuitive organizations, on the other hand, focus on the big picture rather than the detail. They are usually able to see new opportunities and may find others to manage routine tasks and obligations. Outsourcing food services, benefits or building maintenance are all examples in health care. Intuitive organizations often encourage change, frequently of a transformational nature. Bridges describes them as believing that "the future can be created" while emphasizing "purpose and vision."

Examples of health care organizations that we have found to have a Sensing preference contained within their character include:

• A clinic dedicated to treating patients with infertility. The staff collect large quantities of specialist data, run routine tests and advise on a structured series of treatments. They continually review their results and only introduce new methods which fit within their existing model, following careful study of findings elsewhere.
• An operating room, used for orthopedic surgery. The staff pride themselves on their safety record and continue to develop methods of checking instrument numbers before and after surgery as part of routine safety checks.

Examples of health care organizations that we have found to have an Intuitive preference contained within their character include:

• A management section of a new clinic, set up by a specialist in pain control who found it impossible to test his ideas in a mainstream medical setting. The clinic's major objective is to discover new methods of pain control using both traditional and non-traditional techniques.

- A walk-in service for patients with mental health problems, providing care based on the latest research. The service providers believe that the patients have usually tried all the current treatments without success, which makes the use of cutting-edge techniques acceptable, if occasionally risky.

## Thinking and Feeling

The Thinking and Feeling dimension can be observed in the ways in which an organization handles information and reaches conclusions.

Organizations with a Thinking character are likely to make decisions based on non-personal logic. They tend to value objective analysis and the expression of honest criticism, which they see as leading to greater effectiveness. As employers they encourage competence or, as Bridges puts it, they encourage employees "to live up to expectations."

Feeling organizations are more likely to make decisions based on people-centered values. They tend to value people over objectivity and believe that individual encouragement is the greatest motivator. Feeling organizations may consider the upholding of person-centered values and harmony between all of the people – staff and clientele – to be of the utmost importance.

Examples of health care organizations that we have found to have a Thinking preference contained within their character include:

- The specialist accounts department of a large health care provider, set up to investigate methods of improving value-for-money in service delivery. In the initial stages the accountants became aware of the potential for fraud and developed a sub-division to deal with this problem.
- An independent hospital board of a clinic which provides routine day surgery at fixed-cost rates. The clinic has as its objective the provision of an efficient, cost-effective service to users. The staff are encouraged to be efficient and monthly meetings are held to review progress as measured by the standards set by the board.

Examples of health care organizations that we have found to have a Feeling preference contained within their character include:

- A hospice set up in a country location with a legacy from a local person. The building was designed to provide a peaceful, caring atmosphere. The staff were recruited by a non-executive board whose brief was to select "caring" individuals. The objective is to provide holistic care based on personal values. The paid staff are supported by unpaid volunteers, most of whom have themselves been bereaved. The staff office is adorned with "thank you" cards from families of patients who have died.

* A counseling service developed to support health care professionals experiencing stress. The counselors meet regularly to share cases and concerns and to find ways of providing a better service for their patients. They are also involved in developing an educational program for managers entitled "Caring for the Carers."

## Judging and Perceiving

This dimension provides information about how organizations prefer to interact with the outer world, whether in a decisive, planned mode or an open, spontaneous manner.

Organizations with a Judging character are likely to consider decisions and task completion to be of the utmost importance. Their downside may be to make, on occasion, premature decisions based on insufficient data. The standards, time-frames and structures of a Judging organization are likely to be very clear.

Organizations with a Perceiving preference are likely to be more flexible, opportunistic or *ad hoc* in their information gathering and decision making. They may find decisions, or closure, less satisfying. Their downside may be in collecting more information or more options than necessary, potentially wasting time and resources.

Examples of health care organizations that we have found to have a Judging preference contained within their character include:

* A laboratory dealing with blood and tissue samples. The aim of the department is to return all routine tests within 24 hours and standards have been written to that effect. When the performance drops below the standard an inquiry is immediately launched to uncover the reason.
* A pharmacy department handling prescription forms which drew up standards to ensure accuracy in dispensing and set target times for patients to receive their medication. The pharmacy staff tend to be critical of local doctors for both their delay in providing prescriptions and errors in prescribing.

Examples of health care organizations that we have found to have a Perceiving preference contained within their character include:

- A practice of doctors who formed a co-operative to free themselves from what they saw as intrusive management behavior when they were part of a large managed unit. They provide a flexible, walk-in service for patients rather than an appointment system. The aims of their service tend to change and evolve according to perceived local need.
- A small team of specialist nurses who set up an inter-disciplinary approach to caring for the elderly. They believed that the most important service they could provide was one that was responsive and patient-led. They did not, therefore, book many pre-planned visits, allowing the patients to take more responsibility for their own decisions.

## The sixteen MBTI types

You may have reached a decision as to which of the sixteen MBTI types best describes your organization. If you refer back to Table 1.3 (see p. 26) the descriptions set out for individuals may well assist you in clarifying your thinking.

How can this information be of help? It can, just as on an individual basis, help organizations to recognize their strengths and potential blind spots. The examples describe organizations whose central character is reflected to a degree in what they do – for example, the Thinking department involved in investigating fraud; the Feeling organization providing direct, hands-on care.

The Thinking and Feeling dimension stands out as being particularly important in health care. Our experience is that a very large percentage of nurses and other health care workers involved in providing direct care prefer Feeling. In palliative care, this figure can reach 80–90 per cent. When Myers did her initial research on nurses in the US (Myers 1980), she discovered a 78 per cent preference for Feeling among her sample. More often than not, the Feeling preference is accompanied by Sensing. In Myers' study the figure was 44 per cent for Sensing and Feeling. What tends to happen is that people with preferences for Thinking, and possibly Intuition, become involved in a specialist, educational or managerial capacity. Thus, a Thinking and Feeling type mix is achieved overall but often in a way that can lead to conflict within parts of the organizations.

The important thing to recognize is that a relatively even number of patients will have Thinking or Feeling preferences. In the US the percentages are approximately 40 per cent Thinking and 60 per cent Feeling, and in the UK, 45.9 per cent Thinking and 54.1 per cent Feeling (Briggs Myers *et al.* 1998).

If there are problems in valuing one preference over another, especially if valuing accentuates organizational or team problems, this may not lead to the best patient communication and care.

These issues highlight the value of examining not only individual and team preferences but also that of the organization.

## Exercise

1   Think of an organization that is familiar to you. Use the information presented in this section to try and identify which preferences describe this organization in MBTI terms.
2   Identify what the organization does well and not so well.
3   Look for links between these lists and the perceived MBTI preferences.
4   List ideas for possible improvement.

## Summary

In this section we have introduced and developed the idea that organizations, like individuals, tend to have observable type preferences. We identified the issues that contribute to the development of those preferences and described typical health care organizations in order to illustrate the link between type and organizational character. Finally, we outlined the advantages of understanding character in this way in that it can help organizations to recognize and work to their strengths and identify areas for development.

## THE MANAGEMENT OF CHANGE IN TEAMS AND ORGANIZATIONS

Earlier on in this chapter, we indicated that meetings are a fact of life. This applies equally to change. Change is an ever-accelerating force in our lives and there is little doubt that the way in which we handle change differs in line with our type preference. In the previous section, for example, it was quite clear that the organizations with a preference for Intuition tended to adopt an experimental approach, with all its benefits and liabilities; while those more inclined toward Sensing were prone to follow a traditional approach, with its own benefits and liabilities. In this section, we will examine a theory of change and how type might affect the different ways in which we manage change, whether as individuals, teams or organizations.

In his book *Managing Transitions – Making the Most of Change*, Bridges (1991) defined a number of identifiable stages in the overall process of change. This work was further developed in *The Challenge of Change in Organizations* (Barger and Kirby 1995) which defined the links between the theory of Bridges and the MBTI. The authors compared organizational change to the journey undertaken by the US pioneers in the mid-1800s who traveled two thousand miles from the middle of North America to its west coast (Missouri to Oregon), for land or a better life. No doubt many left their homes with great optimism in their hearts but in time these pioneers reacted to the trials of the challenge posed in crossing the Rocky Mountains in a way that many of us might recognize:

> I had no idea it would be so hard!
> Maybe we could go back?
> Maybe the old days weren't so bad?
> Can we go round the mountains, avoid them in some way?
>
> (Barger and Kirby 1995)

As this example demonstrates, change can often bring with it a sense of regret, fear or foreboding – or maybe a mixture of all three.

Bridges (1991) believes that it is the process of "transition" – literally or figuratively crossing the Rocky Mountains – which people can find difficult to manage in times of change. He identifies that process as being made up of three parts:

* Endings
* The neutral zone
* New beginnings

## Endings

When we change a system, something is lost. We need to identify what might be lost and by whom. If it is something that appears simple at a strategic level – for example, a need to reorganize office space – we may need to consider the effect on individuals who might have to move. For some people such a move may include losses, for others gains, but everyone involved is leaving something behind.

For example, a clinic installed a dishwasher and a number of volunteer helpers were very upset. The manager was perplexed, she thought a dishwasher would be helpful. In fact the feelings expressed by the volunteers included believing that their work in washing dishes was being criticized, that they were not as important as they had been and, no doubt, they missed the opportunity for conversation which took place while doing the dishes together. This was an "ending" which had been overlooked.

In general terms we tend not to enjoy endings and can overlook their importance.

## The neutral zone

This is the stage that Bridges describes as being "between trapezes" or in "no-man's land." To give a simple example of this phase: we are aware that our health care organization has developed a new strategic plan designed to meet the needs of an increasingly elderly population. However, we must wait for the consultation process to take place before knowing the effect on our department.

We are in limbo and often feel uneasy during this time. This is possibly the time when the people involved in the change need the most support. It may also be a time of dissent. In terms of patient care the neutral zone is common – the time between realizing "something is wrong with me" and the diagnosis, the time waiting for treatment, or even the time after treatment waiting to see if "it worked." One of the clearest examples would be a patient needing a major organ transplant who has to wait for the right donor.

Bridges points out that, because it is uncomfortable, this stage is often denied or rushed. It is also a time of potential creativity if it is handled well:

> The positive aspect often is the individual's and the organization's best chance for creativity and development.
>
> (Bridges 1991)

When change is in process, accepted practice can be re-evaluated. For example, it can provide opportunity for people to develop new skills or to re-examine ways in which an organization is run. During this time "listening for understanding," not agreeing or disagreeing, may be the key behavior needed. Chapter 8 will detail a model for creating dialogue that leads to committed action.

## New beginnings

To continue with the example of a strategic plan, the new beginning may be signaled by the publication of the plan and reorganization of staff. We are part of an enlarged team, we have a new leader. Although she seems very nice, maybe more experienced than the one who has left, part of "us" remains with the previous configuration and leader. Like the pioneers there are times when we want to go back.

The success of the new beginning depends largely on the attention that was paid to the first stages. Where issues were ignored, people tend to focus on the ending for a long time, they mourn what was lost and continue to believe that the new configuration will not work.

> Beginnings, after all, establish once and for all that an ending was real.
>
> (Bridges 1991)

## Celebration

Although celebration is not a defined part of the Bridges process, it is an important consideration. The celebration marks the end of a period of change.

Sadly, not all changes end in celebration. Often there are too many painful and unresolved issues remaining, some of which might have been prevented or resolved through an understanding of type theory.

## Type Theory and the Management of Change

Knowledge of type theory can often help people to better cope with change. It is important to clarify the fact that everyone can deal with change, it is simply that they may do so differently. The ways in which people of different types manage change follows a pattern which you may now find familiar.

In workshops, when people with different preferences are asked what they need during a period of change, the results are predictable. Extraverts want to talk about it, Introverts prefer time to think. Those with a Sensing preference focus on the present and need factual information. They tend to question whether change is necessary and, if so, how it would work in practice. Intuitives look to the future possibilities, the broader view, and tend to neglect practical implications. Thinking types check for logical outcomes, while Feeling types are more likely to reflect on the people who will be affected. Judging types tend to be uneasy if indecision is involved or no plan has been laid out, while those with a preference for Perceiving enjoy examining options or troubleshooting. They may find a plan confining and want to modify as "necessary."

The greatest contrast, however, in the management of change seems to exist between those with preferences for Intuition and Perceiving (NP) and those with a preference for Sensing and Judging (SJ). The combination of Intuition and Perceiving (Big Picture and Joy of Processing) seems to truly enjoy the process of change. Bridges (1993) describes the NPs with whom he has worked in times of change as saying, "This is kind of interesting . . . there aren't deadlines here . . . it is a state of pure possibility. . . ." On the other hand, the SJs, who combine a preference for Specifics and Joy of Closure, tend to value what is. When caught in the process of change, Bridges describes them as likely to be tapping on the table. They may ask, "When are we going to get out of this, is there any way we can speed up this process, when does it finish . . . can we shorten it?"

What tends to happen is that the people who enjoy the idea of change are often the ones who initiate it. They may not, however, be as gifted when is comes to practical implementation or conserving what existed. It is exactly here that type is most useful:

• Acknowledge your own preferences and the advantages they bring.
• Consciously move into other type modes to gain greater understanding of what is needed to successfully move through a change.
• Value and use the diversity of preferences.

An understanding of type helps to establish a dialogue that will create the strongest end result.

Having summarized the stages of change and the potential implications of type theory we will examine a case history. It describes a situation which did not go well and where the participants appear to have different MBTI preferences.

A nurse training officer with preferences for ENTP wanted to change the way in which patient care was recorded. A new system, radically different from the existing model, was being recommended in professional bulletins. It was hailed as a wonderful innovation. The training officer discussed it with a manager and then chose three units in which to implement the system on a trial basis. The managers of those units all presented in SJ modes, ISFJ, ESFJ and ESTJ. The current system of recording involved detailed information about the patient and a daily note of progress. The system was the same for every patient. The new system required the identification of problems to be addressed, relevant details only and no need for daily recording.

The training officer explained to the staff what would be required and worked with the units when the new method was introduced. On the first two units, it went quite well but, on the third, it did not. There was an undercurrent of hostility and a lack of open co-operation, described by the training officer as "repressed hostility" (Allen 1996). The training officer tried ever harder to convince the staff of the value of the new system, asking herself "How could they doubt me, why [can] they not see that it has worked elsewhere, could save time, and is more professional?" (Allen 1996). Eventually the training officer discovered that the manager was secretly maintaining the old recording system in parallel with the new and keeping it hidden. Worse still, it transpired that the second unit to implement the change was doing likewise.

The training officer realized, too late, that the staff had no confidence in the new system and "were fearful of jettisoning the tried and tested" (Allen 1996). The trial ended in failure and when the training officer met the ward manager some ten years later it was apparent that feelings still ran high.

## Case analysis

In analyzing this case study, we need to look at each of Bridges' stages – Endings, Neutral zone, New beginnings – and the part type may have played in the outcome.

## Endings

The unit managers had been using the same system of recording throughout their professional careers. The manager who found the change most difficult appeared to work generally in the mode of Extraversion, Sensing, Feeling and Judging; with a preference for the personal and traditional approach, and an affinity with the tried and tested. She also wanted to please the doctors with whom she worked by having the required information at hand. The training officer had preferences for Extraversion, Intuition, Thinking and Perceiving. She liked searching for new ideas and was excited by change that made logical sense to her.

In terms of dealing with endings and the losses involved, Barger and Kirby (1995) describe potential difficulties for ENTPs as including difficulty with "People who want to hang on to the past." For ESFJs the problems can be quite different and include "Loss of certainty, of knowing what's expected."

In the light of this information, how could they have handled this stage differently?

The training officer could have:

- Listened fully to the needs and concerns expressed by the staff and unit manager, which included anxieties of a legal nature.
- Acknowledged that this was a big change and worked with the staff to set a work plan that approached it incrementally.
- Taken time to go through the new system while reviewing the current system, together with the unit managers. They would have found that there were omissions in the new method – for example, no provision in the paper work for things that had to be recorded. The new forms could have been adapted.

The managers could have:

- Listened to truly understand the training officer's ideas.
- Been more open to examining the new system.
- Been more honest and constructive in their concerns, producing hard information about the shortcomings of the new paperwork and insisting that their concerns be acknowledged.

## The neutral zone

There was a period between the agreement that the change would take place and the actual implementation. Very little discussion took place; the ward manager hid her concerns from the training officer but shared them with the staff. The training officer did not see there was anything to talk about. In this transitional period, Barger and Kirby describe ENTPs having as their focus "What they can make out of this opportunity." The training officer saw this as the beginning of a change for the whole hospital. ESFJs, however, tend to focus more on, "Creating structure and security . . . [and] keeping harmony, keeping everyone happy."

In the light of this information, how could they have handled this stage differently?

The training officer could have:

- Given more time and attention to the unit concerned, examined the detail.
- Considered the people involved in the change.
- Worked with the managers on a plan to evaluate the key purposes of a recording system.
- Set up check-points to evaluate a new system, creating the mechanism for and expectation of open dialogue to meet agreed-upon needs.
- Made scheduled times to listen to, understand, not agree or disagree with, their questions and concerns.
- Concentrated on seeing the change from the managers' point of view.
- Involved the staff in problem solving those issues that were key.

The managers could have:

- Listened for understanding of, not to agree or disagree with, the training officer's reasons for promoting the change.
- Shared their anxieties with the training officer.
- Asked for and worked on a plan to evaluate the key purposes of a recording system.
- Worked out a list of concerns in discussion with the staff and shared them with the training officer in a set of ongoing meetings throughout the "new beginnings" phase.

### New beginnings

The case study illustrates how difficult the new beginning actually was. Relationships were strained and people were polarized. In response to her fears about the safety of the new system, the manager ran two systems, one to preserve superficial harmony and one to ensure safety. This is something Bridges recognizes:

> People won't dare stop doing anything. They'll try to do all the old things *and* the new things. After a while they'll burn themselves out with the overload.
>
> (Bridges 1993)

This is exactly what happened. All parties suffered from extreme stress, which for the ENTP was expressed in enormous and lasting self-doubt and indecision over future projects. The ESFJ became more closely allied to her own staff and other managers. She was exhausted and angry.

### *Celebration*

Understandably, there was no celebration and unfortunately no review of the situation.

## Exercise

1    Think of a time of change within your organization. Did it go well, or not so well?
2    Make notes about that time using the three headings, Endings, Neutral zone and New beginnings.
3    Use your understanding of the MBTI type preferences to look for behavior cues of the principal people.
4    Note how type preferences either helped or hindered in this case.
5    Lastly, note anything you feel might have been done differently. Try to use all function modes, though you may be drawn to one or two:
  •    What were the facts of the situation (Sensing)?
  •    What were the possibilities or options (Intuition)?
  •    For each, analyze the pros and cons (Thinking).
  •    For each, consider the people impact, short and long range (Feeling).

## Summary

Change is, as we have said, an essential part of life. It can be exciting and productive or it can be stressful and negative. In this section we have described the change process, as identified by Bridges, before identifying links between response to change and MBTI preferences.

The case study concerning the training officer provided an opportunity for analysis using both systems and helped to illustrate the fact that a greater understanding of both the process of change itself and of individual type differences may well improve the outcome.

This case also illustrates the need for an overall understanding of how to:

- Assess needs
- Closely consider perspectives
- Create an environment of real listening for understanding

As a result new possibilities can emerge together with commitment for action and implementation.

Too often all types hold onto their own perspective, forgetting that in order for change to occur and "stick," all points of view must be considered. Increasingly, organizations are becoming aware that "Do it because I say so" is too expensive a way to try to implement change. If it ever did work, it does not work in today's organizations which require flexible, co-ordinated and rapid responses. Chapter 8, "Creating committed action," will outline in more detail a structure for creating dialogue and change at the organizational level as well as at the team and individual level.

# 7 Type – a tool for personal and professional development

In the first two chapters of the book we examined the basic theory contained within the MBTI and put it to use by introducing the practical system of FLEX Care. In the later chapters, we considered many case studies and specialist applications of the type theory. This chapter will address how an understanding of the interaction or dynamics of type elements can lead to an even deeper understanding of self and our ability to appreciate and work effectively with others.

This chapter will:

- Describe ways of working with type in a developmental manner, cautioning against the misuse of type as a label.
- Apply type to creative problem-solving.
- Outline ways in which an understanding of the MBTI can enhance professional development.
- Explain ways in which type theory can help understand and manage stress.

## Type as preference, not a label

Those involved in introducing the MBTI have a great responsibility to "model" both the constructive use and language of type. The choice of words and openness to acknowledging the strengths and limitations of the MBTI are crucial at the introductory stage. It was for this purpose that type was compared to a "sixteen-room house" in Chapter 1. The idea of movement between rooms as opposed to being "stuck in a box" is in itself liberating and consistent with Jung's theory:

> It is not the purpose of psychological typology to classify human beings into categories – this in itself would be pointless.
>
> (Jung 1971)

It is all too easy to fall into the trap of "labeling." The following extract, which is taken from *I'm Not Crazy, I'm Just Not You* (Pearman and Albritton 1997), provides an example of positive use of type language. In the chapter entitled "Sorting among Sensing and Intuition" the authors write about their respective sons:

> Roger's son, Luke, and Sarah's son, Wells, have been best buddies from the start; they are very close in age. We suspect that Luke gets his information from his senses, while Wells seems to be more attuned to intuitive messages.

The title itself gives an air of flexibility; this is the start of an exploration. Furthermore, the way this section is written, using words such as "seems" and "suspect," begins to paint a picture of the possible preferences of these two boys, without "labeling" them – "Luke *is* a sensing type, Wells *is* an intuitive." These are, unfortunately, phrases in common usage. The authors continue to illustrate their initial statement in the form of a story:

> One beautiful day when they were around four years old, they were outside swinging together, side by side. Luke was joyously exclaiming and reporting about all his sensory experiences: "The breeze is in my hair and feels cool! The sky is blue and so is my toy train and so are my pants! The grass is green and tickles my feet! The trees are green too!" Wells, not to be outdone, shouted, "The trees are pushing the sky!" Luke's rejoinder was the sort many people preferring Intuition feel they get from pragmatists, "No, they're not."

This section demonstrates the ways in which two children appear to perceive the same scene in a very different way. It also provides a sense that neither method is better than the other. This is the kind of understanding that can help us begin to use the language of type responsibly. Finally, there is a gentle humor in the telling – working with type can produce the healthiest form of fun if used appropriately. It can act as a balance against taking it all too seriously.

A simple shift of language further illustrates the differences between preference and label. Try inserting your own type preference into the following sentences. "I am an ESFJ" versus "I have an ESFJ preference." The first sentence labels, the second puts type into the proper perspective of using all type elements while preferring some.

Appropriate language and an exploratory approach to the use of type theory reflect the wish of Myers herself:

> The merit of the theory . . . is that it enables us to expect specific personality differences in particular people and to cope with the people and differences in a constructive way.
>
> (Myers 1980)

## Creative problem-solving using the functions

One important aspect of an individual's ability to call upon all aspects of type is to recognize how one prefers to take in information and come to a conclusion. In order to put this idea into practice we need to return to the four functions:

- *Sensing and Intuition*: how one prefers to take in information (the Perceiving functions)
- *Thinking and Feeling*: how one prefers to come to conclusions (the Judging functions)

As we have previously explained, one Perceiving function and one Judging function are generally one's favorites or preferences.

It is helpful to use the following questions, which relate to the four functions, when problem-solving or reflecting on a situation:

| | | |
|---|---|---|
| 1 | What are the *facts*? | Sensing |
| 2 | What are the *possibilities*? | Intuition |
| 3 | What are the *logical options*? | Thinking |
| 4 | What are the *implications for people*? | Feeling |

Our overall tendency would be to use our preferred functions before, or in place of, the others. For example, those people with preferences for Intuition and Thinking may confine themselves solely to possibilities and logical options, thus running the risk of overlooking an important fact or personal implication. By applying the type framework, we ensure that we gain the advantage of all four functions, as the following case study demonstrates. The method lends itself to both individual and group working. It can provide structure for the individual and the opportunity for a group to share their strengths. This case study illustrates how this framework of type functions was used by an individual in a problem-solving exercise.

Marie worked in a commissioning department of a company that owned health care clinics. No new clinic or development of an existing service could proceed without the consent of her department.

A new clinic had been built and was in the process of moving to completion. Marie's colleague, Bill, had been leading this initiative since it was in his area of expertise. Marie knew that there had been tensions between Bill and Jan, the chief executive of the project, and that Bill mistrusted the chief executive.

Out of the blue, Marie found herself in the midst of this situation. She received a call telling her that the agreed commissioning date had arrived and no formal agreement had been received. Bill was on leave abroad, he had left her without instructions and she now had to work with an angry chief executive.

How could she resolve this situation, using the framework of type functions?

### What are the facts?

By listening to the Chief Executive and referring to Bill's files, she discovered that:

- This was the agreed date.
- Staff had been hired and were due to commence work.
- Patients were scheduled for admission and treatment in two days' time.
- The ground floor of the two-story clinic was complete and satisfactory.
- The upper floor was almost complete.
- The elevator had been installed but not tested and certified for safe use.

### What are the possibilities?

Using her own experience, she could see that she had a number of options:

- To delay the opening of the clinic.
- To allow it to open fully and trust that the outstanding work would be satisfactorily completed.
- To consider ways of opening a portion of the clinic while retaining control over the areas that had not been completed – the obvious possibility being to open the ground floor.

### What are the logical options of each possibility?

Having identified the facts and possibilities, she examined their pros and cons in turn:

- If she delayed the opening of the clinic, she would not be involved in any risk. She could ensure that the clinic was complete before opening. On the other hand, her department appeared to have made a mistake and she felt it should do what it could to rectify it. She also considered the position of the staff and patients. How fair would it be to delay things? She came to the conclusion that the needs of the clinic outweighed the risk involved, and felt that she could work to minimize any risk.
- While it might seem an easy option to agree to open the whole clinic, she knew that, once she did this, her department would not have the same level of authority to ensure the remaining work was done. Therefore, she might run an unacceptable risk, especially given the fact that Bill had concerns about the integrity of the chief executive.
- She therefore examined the option of opening part of the clinic. The ground floor was complete but the upper floor and elevator were not. She checked how many patients were expected and discovered that only a percentage of the ground floor would be occupied. On balance, she decided that this was probably the best logical option.

### How will this affect the people involved?

Before she concluded her deliberations, she considered the position of the people involved:

- *The chief executive*: she felt that the chief executive had been let down by her department and that she should help her as much as possible. She also had to bear in mind the existence of friction before this event and could see that she might in fact improve relations by being seen to act practically and positively.

- *The staff*: staff had been hired to open this clinic and she wanted to support them and start them with a positive work experience.
- *The patients*: patients had been scheduled into the clinic and would be disappointed and upset by the delay. Her priority was that they be treated in a safe and timely manner.
- *Bill*: she was annoyed with Bill for leaving her in this position and knew that before she could put her plan into action she would have to consult Bill's departmental manager who might want to take the matter further.
- *Herself*: she acknowledged a mixture of personal feelings. She was pleased that she could help the clinic and the department by working creatively with a chief executive who could be difficult, and in this case had every right to be. She saw a possibility of better working relations in the future.
- She also acknowledged that she would have to come to a mutual understanding with Bill when he came back. She honestly evaluated her emotions and found she wanted to express her annoyance and also avoid blame, martyrdom or distrust. A smooth, trusting, straightforward working relationship with him was most important over the long term.

While the case study describes a real case, it is given as a model to demonstrate the relevance of applying all four functions to the decision-making process. This ensures that an individual with, for example, a preference for Intuition and Feeling is conscious of the need to ensure that facts and logical options are explored as well as the possibilities and people issues.

This simple method can, as mentioned earlier, also be used in team situations. It can help people with different type preferences to work creatively together. For example, each team member can reflect on the task, using this framework. The team can then come together to brainstorm the four elements. Understanding the type preference in the team can help members to predict their preferred methods of interaction and avoid inadvertently forgetting important issues.

It is also important for individuals to add comments related to all four of the functions contained in the framework. This helps avoid the potential for labeling comments such as: "Well, you are the thinking person, so you can do the logical options."

Used carefully, this model can allow each member to use their strengths while at the same time encouraging individuals to develop their less preferred functions.

## Using type for enhanced professional insight

One of the greatest gifts contained within the Myers-Briggs framework is the possibility for personal development. Thinking back to
the "sixteen-room house," we have already seen that, far from being
contained in one room, we are free to explore the whole house.
However, we often find our own room to be very cozy and secure
and might need encouragement to widen our experience.

The problem with remaining in this one room is that we are more
likely to believe and act as though our own type preference is best.
Each type combination has potential benefits and blindspots. If we
communicate with someone with similar type preferences to our own,
we may have the same blindspots. The communication flows easily
enough and it is often only in hindsight or on reflection that we see
what might have been missed.

### *Case study 1 – the potential pitfalls of "matching" functions*

Having the same or different type preferences does not automatically lead to success or difficulty. Understanding one's own
preferences and how they contribute to personal patterns of behavior
is the key to effectiveness.

We can now look at a situation where it is possible that a practitioner missed reference to one of the four functions. The practitioner
concerned has preferences for Extraversion, Intuition, Thinking and
Perceiving (ENTP).

---

I had a new patient in the Day Hospice, who was referred
for social support. He was due to commence out-patient
chemotherapy and was, at the same time, the main carer of
his wife who has Alzheimer's disease. He was asking about
the treatment, its effects and side-effects. As we talked it
seemed he wanted all the information he could obtain in order
to prepare himself for the effects of the treatment and to work
out how it would affect his life. I felt pleased that he had
asked me as I used to administer chemotherapy and felt it
was an area I could discuss well. I wanted to tell him exactly
what the treatment was, how it is given and its potential side-
effects and what to do about them.

> I asked him what he had already been told and then gave him the information he asked for. I asked him how he felt about his treatment, but he did not want to discuss it, he only wanted factual information. At the end of our interview, he was apparently satisfied and stated he was less anxious about the treatment.

The nurse in this case presented this exchange as a positive case study. When asked why she considered it to be so she replied as follows:

• The patient wanted "hard information" and I was able to give it.
• I felt competent to help the patient.
• I feel the patient was given what he wanted, i.e. information.

The practitioner's MBTI preferences are:

• Big Picture
• Logical Implications

She reported that she assessed the mode of the patient to be:

• Specifics
• Logical Implications

Reflecting on the written study, she could see that she had responded to the need for "specifics" fully by giving him the information he was seeking. She had also covered the "logical implications" of the treatment, the side-effects.

The area of personal implications was touched on very briefly, "I asked him how he felt about his treatment."

On reflection, she thought that she may have been caught up in an area in which she is comfortable – knowledge of the treatment process – and may not have fully covered his personal fears and anxieties. This seemed particularly important as the referral was for social support. In hindsight, she wondered if the fact that both she and the patient may have been more comfortable with "Logical Implications" might have prevented more discussion about the personal impact of the illness. She also realized that she did not address the family issues, that is, the "Big Picture" of his family relationships.

She considered other possible ways in which she might have made more progress. Rather than restrict her query to how the patient felt about the treatment she realized she could have asked, "How are you getting on at home?"

Alternatively, she could have been more proactive, "I guess it must be difficult for you, coping with the treatment as well as caring for your wife, how is she, by the way?"

The exercise was of great value to her because she recognized the potential oversight for herself simply as a result of writing it out and applying the framework of the four functions.

It is important to understand that it may not be possible, or even desirable, to cover all areas in one conversation. Building trust and credibility with that patient by matching their type mode is a necessary first step. It may help, however, to note the patient's behavior cues together with unexplored areas in the record, or to discuss the matter with co-workers. Finally, it is important to think through what might have been left out of the treatment plan.

What the case demonstrates is:

- It is important to be aware of how patient behavior modes match to the type preferences of the professional.
- There is value in covering all four functions, either at the time or at the next possible opportunity.

The potential for missing important issues when the professional's preferences match those of the patient may not always give rise to problems; it depends a great deal, as we have already discovered, on the awareness of the professional concerned.

### Case study 2 – using matching preferences to good effect

The second case study again relates to a professional and patient with apparently similar type preferences. This case was provided by a nurse specialist, interviewing a patient who was due to undergo surgery. The nurse's preferences are for Introversion, Sensing, Thinking and Judging (ISTJ).

I was interviewing a 42-year-old woman with breast cancer. I wasn't with her at diagnosis so I had been unable to assess her reaction and to know what questions had been asked and her level of involvement. Being at diagnosis also helps see the interaction of the significant other at this stage. I was seeing her to discuss her diagnosis and her surgical treatment options. I was with the patient and her husband.

I wanted background information, the type of cancer and where it was situated in the breast. I also wanted to know her obstetric and family history and whether she had any other family members who have had cancer. I am asking myself whether she wants to be involved in the decision-making process, how supportive her husband will be, how she views her body (this is difficult to assess at diagnosis). I intended to assess her methods of coping.

I made a brief note of what we could do; discuss the diagnosis and the treatment options. I checked that this was OK and asked for any questions. I asked how she was feeling about things. She was very matter of fact. I mentioned that she seemed calm and she said she was at the moment. She was fact-finding and the emotions would come later. She said she wanted to stay in control. We discussed how the lump had been found; she used the word "cancer" straight away and seemed quite at ease with that. We discussed the surgical options and she had a definite preference for breast conservation rather than mastectomy. We discussed in detail the scarring and what would be removed and other effects. Often people can't take all this on board but she could and wanted it.

This patient came wanting factual information; she had obtained some information from a variety of sources. She had developed a very effective coping strategy and has needed minimal support. I did see her once more and she thanked me for my help. When I said I only saw her once, she said I had given her what she wanted. We were able at a later date to discuss more sensitive issues more easily than we might have done because of this rapport.

The nurse presented the case study as positive. She explained her reasons as follows:

- The patient was able to articulate what she wanted, i.e. factual information.

- She had already considered the diagnosis and was not afraid to use the word "cancer."
- I was able to give an unusually large amount of information without overloading her.
- She appeared to be coping realistically with the situation.

The practitioner's own MBTI preferences are:

- Specifics
- Logical Implications

She reported that she assessed the mode of the patient to be:

- Specifics
- Logical Implications

Reflecting on the case study it was apparent that the personal implications had been addressed in that the patient was asked how she was feeling. When a "matter of fact" response was received, she probed it further by commenting on the degree of apparent calmness. The patient was then able to acknowledge her own coping process, first information, then feelings. Her feelings were neither ignored, nor were they intruded upon prematurely.

The immediate possibilities were also covered in that the surgical options were explained. The rapport established provided a basis for further conversations about possibilities including sensitive issues such as the risk of recurrence.

### Case study 3 – potential difficulties with non-matching preferences

We now need to consider the learning and developmental potential in two cases where the professional's and the patient's preferences did not match. The first case describes an incident where the outcome was difficult. The professional concerned, a specialist community nurse, has preferences for Extraversion, Sensing, Feeling and Perceiving (ESFP).

My patient was a 29-year-old woman, a single mother of a 5-year-old boy living together in an apartment. She had had a seizure, which had led to investigations, scans and so on. She had been diagnosed as having a brain tumor. Unfortunately, she had read about this in a letter before being told. The tumor was of a lower grade, which may respond to treatment. Her doctor asked me to visit because she had requested that someone talk to her. It was on a Friday and so I went right away.

I felt slightly anxious about going because the doctor had said she was not coping well and was not the sort to cope with waiting. I wanted to ease some of her anxiety by giving more information and to support her by being a sounding board. The two of us were sitting together.

I listened to her ranting and raving. I told her I would find out more about the scan, when it would be, because the scan was the key to whether she needed more treatment. I could not get a date, just reassurance that the scan would be done. I gave her a helpline number so that she could get a booklet on her disease, as I did not have one with me. This meant I could not go through it with her.

I thought I had reassured her about the scan and by getting her information about the disease. However, when I went back, she had had the scan and was waiting for the results. She had read the booklet and realized from the information it contained that her tumor was malignant. I had not been sure of this. She was very angry with me and thought I had let her down – had not put my cards on the table. She was angry with everyone else too. It was very difficult for me.

The nurse presented this as a negative incident and when asked why she said:

- The patient wanted factual information I didn't have.
- She had already experienced learning about her condition by reading a letter, rather than being told by her doctor.
- I wasn't able to schedule an appointment there and then.
- I responded to a cry for help without being aware of the full situation. I could have checked a reference book before leaving.

- By giving her the helpline number, I inadvertently repeated the mis-take which had occurred when she read her diagnosis in a letter.

The case study highlighted a well-known pattern in her professional life where she would respond, almost without thinking, to a personal need.
The practitioner's own MBTI preferences are:

- Specifics
- Feeling

She reported that she assessed the mode of the patient as:

- Specifics
- Logical Implications

There is one further type issue here – that of Judging and Perceiving. It appears that the patient had a Judging preference, the nurse a Perceiving preference. This came out in the follow-up discussion. The nurse described the patient as a "control freak," always planning miles ahead. This, of course, was not the way in which, as a Perceiving type, she ran her life.

The anger expressed by the patient, after what the nurse saw as her best effort, was painful for her but she did recognize the need to take time to use her preference for specifics to check her facts in the future. This case brings out one other piece of information that a professional can use to understand self and others. Notice how the nurse describes the patient with a negatively connoted phrase: "control freak." Though patient type mode may not be the only reason we use a negatively connoted phrase to describe an individual, it is often a clue that we are experiencing a difference in type. This realization often helps us to gain needed perspective on any indi-vidual and thus enables us to better address their needs and our own.

### Case study 4 – using non-matching preferences to good effect

We can now turn to a situation in which the professional and the patient had different preferences but where the contrasts were used to positive effect.

The professional concerned is a nurse, working on a surgical unit. The nurse has preferences for Extraversion, Intuition, Thinking and Perceiving (ENTP).

I had been looking after the same patient off and on for a number of years. I really liked him. He was cheerful, warm-hearted and we had intelligent conversations. He was a pharmacist and someone who took a positive interest in his own condition and always liked to hear the details of his treatment. He came in for further surgery and a few days later, when I had left the surgical unit for a few moments, developed complications. He had a pulmonary embolus. A member of staff paged me and I dashed back to the unit.

I was extremely worried, in case he died. I hoped the staff had been able to get a doctor quickly and that I would be able to help. I rushed back to his room, talked to him calmly (although I didn't feel calm at all!). I checked that medical care was on its way and the doctor arrived. I assisted the doctor in administering the treatment, all the time talking calmly to the patient explaining exactly what treatment was being given and what had happened. He was very tense, so I took his hand and said to him quietly that I couldn't go out for two minutes without him causing chaos. I also told him that his wife knew what had happened and was coming to visit. He smiled and relaxed. Afterwards I told him again what had happened and why, and the kind of treatment he would have to undergo both in the short and longer term. He understood all about the drugs, so it was quite easy.

He was a patient with whom I had a very special professional relationship, he trusted me and I respected him. This incident reinforced that and gave me professional satisfaction. His wife, who I also liked a great deal, asked me to their home and I refused politely because I felt it wasn't ethical while I was working at the hospital. When I left to work elsewhere, however, I did visit them and, as it happened, they introduced me to my husband! We laughed about it, I said it was only fair; I looked after him, he found me a husband!

The nurse involved felt that this was a positive incident because:

- I had formed a good relationship with the patient over a number of admissions – he trusted me.
- When he had the pulmonary embolus he was reassured by my

presence and I was able to reassure him on a professional and a personal basis.

- I was able to relax him by using humor but with a light touch.

The practitioner's own MBTI preferences are:

- Big Picture
- Logical Implications

She reported that she assessed the mode of the patient to be:

- Specifics
- Impact on People

Reflecting on the case the nurse could see that she had recognized this patient's need for "relationship" and being known on a personal basis. During the incident, she was able to combine the personal issues – holding his hand and assuring him that his wife was coming to see him – with the logical facts of what had happened and the implications for treatment. She also used humor appropriately. If she had been less sensitive it might have upset the patient further rather than discharging his anxiety. She had also introduced the wider possibilities in terms of future implications.

In summary, the case studies show that it is possible to communicate effectively with patients who have similar or totally different type preferences. The important issues highlighted here are:

- The essential issue is to be aware of our personal type preferences and how we are *likely* to respond in a given situation.
- We are not confined, however, to using only those preferences – we are able to develop and use all preferences.
- We may not be able to cover all aspects in one discussion, indeed it may not be appropriate to do so, but we need a sense of what has been covered and what has been left out.

## Exercise

It may be helpful to work with a colleague while completing this exercise. The nurses who provided the four case studies were asked to relate their information using a Critical Incident method. They found that by sharing the story in the Critical Incident framework they reflected on the incidents in a different and very constructive way. In the following exercise, we provide the questions of the Critical Incident method to structure your thinking.

Think of two interactions that you have been involved in: one where the outcome was good and one where it was unsatisfactory. Describe each one under the following headings:

1   What was the situation?
2   Who was involved?
3   What did you think, feel or want to do in this situation?
4   What did you do?
5   What was the outcome?

Consider these questions:

1   Looking at the functional pairs in particular, what type mode would best describe you in this interaction? (Use Table 3.1 on p. 51) to help with the behavior cues of type mode.)
    Specifics/Impact on People (SF)
    Specifics/Logical Implications (ST)
    Big Picture/ Impact on People (NF)
    Big Picture/Logical Implications (NT)
2   How would you describe the patient's type mode?
3   On which dimensions did you match, and which were not a match? How would you describe the patient's type mode?
4   For the instances where your behavior cues *matched* those of your patient, what were the positive outcomes, what were the negative outcomes?
5   For the instances in which your behavior cues did *not match* those of your patient, what were the positive outcomes, what were the negative outcomes?
6   How might this perspective change your practice in the future?

## TYPE DYNAMICS AND TYPE DEVELOPMENT

This section is designed to introduce and apply a further piece of theory to the case studies and exercises used in this chapter. An understanding of this applied theory will help the practitioner to:

*   Recognize their own type preferences more clearly.
*   Recognize the type mode of their patients more fully.
*   Appreciate the possibility of the development of all functions, both for themselves and their patients.

The term type dynamics refers simply to the way in which the four different preferences in any one of the sixteen types interact with each other. Type development, as we have already seen, relates to the fact that everyone, regardless of type, is able to use and improve the appropriate use of any one of the preferences. An understanding of type dynamics provides a greater depth to working with the MBTI. Each type generally goes through a specific sequence of development related to the functions. For example, someone with INTJ preferences is likely to prefer using their Intuition and Thinking functions. As they grow older and develop more fully, however, they may become more interested in using their Sensing and Feeling functions. The Intuition and Thinking are most likely to remain their first choice but greater access to the other two functions will help them to achieve a greater balance in both their personal and professional lives. In practical terms, for an INTJ, that may mean that they begin to factor in person-centered values such as harmony and empathy. These values become reflected in communication and decision making. They may also begin to recognize the value of the sensory world, in nature and in the details and routine of life at home and at work.

We have already placed great emphasis on the four functions, Sensing, Intuition, Thinking and Feeling. Jung's theory of psychological type included the fact that each of us is able to access all of the functions but that we prefer to use some rather than others. This was demonstrated in the first chapter in the name-signing exercise, where it became clear that we are usually able to use both our right and left hands, but generally use one much more naturally and easily. Jung believed that the functions formed a natural hierarchy, which is set out below:

1    Dominant function
2    Auxiliary function
3    Third function
4    Fourth function

We have used the terms "third" and "fourth" function since they are clear and practical. However, in type literature you may find them referred to as the tertiary and inferior functions. We have chosen to reserve the term "inferior" function to describe a particular case when the fourth function is exhibited during extreme stress.

## The dominant and auxiliary functions

In Jung's view, for each type one of the middle two letters or functions takes the lead in gaining and processing information. This is called the dominant function. If a person's dominant function is Sensing (S), for example, they will naturally be drawn to and interested in the facts of a situation. They will often start an interaction by asking for or recalling the facts. It is as if the information gained by this dominant function forms a foundation from which they can continue. Similarly, a dominant Intuitive is drawn to possibilities, a dominant Thinking type is drawn to logical analysis, and a dominant Feeling type is drawn to consider the people-oriented values at work in a given situation. It is as if this is a "first stop" for the individual. It is important to realize that there is no best first stop, just as there is no best type preference. In addition, dominant preference does not imply "good at." A dominant Sensing type may recount facts inaccurately, just as a dominant Thinking type may engage in poor analysis.

Jung's theory goes on to integrate the other of the middle two letters. For each type, the other of the two letters is known as the auxiliary. It is often a "second stop" for an individual in understanding a situation. Table 7.1 lists the dominant (1) and auxiliary (2) functions for each type. It is important to note that the two functions balance each other. If one is for taking in information – a perceiving function of Sensing or Intuition – the other will be used as a primary basis for coming to a conclusion – a judging function, Thinking or Feeling. Furthermore, the functions will be balanced in their expression: one function will be extraverted – that is we are likely to hear the person talk about this aspect – and the other will be introverted – often thought through quietly.

In Case study 2, the nurse has preferences for ISTJ. From Table 7.1 we can see that her dominant function is Sensing. The account of the interview includes references to wanting "background information, the type of cancer, where it was situated . . . her obstetric and family history." Her priority during the discussion – in keeping with her dominant function – was to establish the facts.

## The third and fourth functions

The third and fourth functions are represented by the two letters, or preferences, which do not appear in the four-letter type designation. For someone with ESFJ preferences, for example, the third and fourth

*Table 7.1*  Hierarchy of functions for each MBTI type

| ISTJ | ISFJ | INFJ | INTJ |
|---|---|---|---|
| 1  Sensing (I) | 1  Sensing (I) | 1  Intuition (I) | 1  Intuition (I) |
| 2  Thinking (E) | 2  Feeling (E) | 2  Feeling (E) | 2  Thinking (E) |
| 3  Feeling | 3  Thinking | 3  Thinking | 3  Feeling |
| 4  Intuition | 4  Intuition | 4  Sensing | 4  Sensing |
| ISTP | ISFP | INFP | INTP |
| 1  Thinking (I) | 1  Feeling (I) | 1  Feeling (I) | 1  Thinking (I) |
| 2  Sensing (E) | 2  Sensing (E) | 2  Intuition (E) | 2  Intuition (E) |
| 3  Intuition | 3  Intuition | 3  Sensing | 3  Sensing |
| 4  Feeling | 4  Thinking | 4  Thinking | 4  Feeling |
| ESTP | ESFP | ENFP | ENTP |
| 1  Sensing (E) | 1  Sensing (E) | 1  Intuition (E) | 1  Intuition (E) |
| 2  Thinking (I) | 2  Feeling (I) | 2  Feeling (I) | 2  Thinking (I) |
| 3  Feeling | 3  Thinking | 3  Thinking | 3  Feeling |
| 4  Intuition | 4  Intuition | 4  Sensing | 4  Sensing |
| ESTJ | ESFJ | ENFJ | ENTJ |
| 1  Thinking (E) | 1  Feeling (E) | 1  Feeling (E) | 1  Thinking (E) |
| 2  Sensing (I) | 2  Sensing (I) | 2  Intuition (I) | 2  Intuition (I) |
| 3  Intuition | 3  Intuition | 3  Sensing | 3  Sensing |
| 4  Feeling | 4  Thinking | 4  Thinking | 4  Feeling |

functions will be Intuition and Thinking (NT). In contrast to the dominant and auxiliary functions, which individuals tend to use most readily, the other two are generally used more rarely or only after conscious reflection. Consequently, there is a tendency for them to be less well developed, although this is not always the case. Just as a person might use their dominant function ineffectively, it is possible to use the third and fourth functions very effectively indeed. The level to which people access and develop these functions varies between individuals. This refers to the process of type development, which is discussed in greater detail in the next section.

If we look at Case study 3, we can see that the nurse has ESFP preferences. From Table 7.1 you will note that her third function is Thinking and her fourth function, Intuition. She describes herself as responding "to a cry for help without being aware of the full position." Before leaving to visit the patient, she does not establish the full picture or take the logical step of checking her reference books about the condition. She was also unaware of the full contents of the booklet that she recommended. Her "first and second" stops were hearing the brief facts of the case (Sensing) and responding to a cry for help (Feeling).

Reflecting on the case, she was able to logically analyze what went wrong (using her third function, Thinking) and put it into the larger picture (her fourth function, Intuition). She stated:

> I believe I respond almost without thinking to a personal need. I want to help! I move into action as soon as possible to comfort and be there. This has led to trouble when I don't stop to consider whether I have all the materials I'll need. It makes me appear scattered and ineffective – the last thing I want.

These cases illustrate the different functions at work. Case study 3 also provides an insight into the value of reflection since it was this activity which allowed the nurse to both identify the context of her difficult case and to use her less preferred functions in so doing.

In the context of this introductory book we have provided only an overview of the subject of type dynamics. In their book *Introduction to Type Dynamics and Development*, Myers and Kirby discuss the subject in greater depth.

## Type development

Having a knowledge of type dynamics can, as explained earlier, help us to identify more easily the ways in which we typically use the different functions. Identifying our dominant and auxiliary functions can help us to understand why we find certain activities more attractive, in that they tend to play to our strengths. Similarly, by identifying our third and fourth functions we can understand reasons why we might feel less at home with other activities.

One important point to re-emphasize here relates to the fact that as adults we all use *all* the functions to some degree in our everyday life. The main difference relates to the level to which we develop and consciously use them.

The following example illustrates the potential development path for someone with ISFJ preferences. First, we need to identify the preferred functions (see Table 7.1):

| | |
|---|---|
| Dominant function: | Sensing (Introverted) |
| Auxiliary function: | Feeling (Extraverted) |

We would expect an ISFJ, therefore, to rely on these functions. This is likely to be reflected in an approach to life characterized in part by an emphasis on practicalities and concern for others. The next function to develop would be the:

Third function:                    Thinking

In developing the third function, an ISFJ might be expected to become more able to use a more logically-structured approach to decision making. They may also become more comfortable stepping back from a situation to apply non-personalized criteria when necessary.

The final stage of type development for an ISFJ relates to the:

Fourth function:                  Intuition

Development of this function would help an ISFJ to put more trust in their own insights or "hunches" and to be more interested in future implications or purpose when making plans or taking decisions.

An understanding of type theory can help people of each type to develop adequate command of all their functions. It can be tempting to use our knowledge of type dynamics as an added excuse for staying the same, "As my fourth function is Thinking, you can't expect me to be logical." If we do this, we are simply "labeling" ourselves and missing a potential opportunity for growth. Many people, however, do not develop, and continue to rely heavily on their dominant function throughout their lives. This tends to lead to a one-sided approach to life. Jung believed that in order to function well in the world we need the balance provided by the dominant and auxiliary functions. Myers (1980) sums this up:

> Although a favorite process can be useful by itself, alone it will not be healthy, safe for society, or ultimately satisfying to the individual, because it lacks balance.

The aim of type development is not to develop all functions equally. Type development is focused much more on balancing, which Pearman and Albritton describe as a "process, not a state of being:"

> If we accept Jung and Myers' definition of type, then it is clear that the balancing of a person's extraverted and introverted energy through the judging and perceiving functions is essential to healthy adaptation and responsiveness. Balancing is an ongoing requirement for a person's continued development and growth.
> (Pearman and Albritton 1997)

It is possible to see examples of the link between work and type development:

- Work situations are often approached by the dominant and auxiliary functions, as illustrated in the earlier case studies. Added to this, we have a tendency – as described in the previous chapter – to work in an environment that acknowledges our strengths.
- Work situations, however, can also often help to develop other functions.
- It is especially useful to have the type framework to understand these challenges and to provide new insight.
- In some cases, differences of type between colleagues may be especially troublesome because the other person seems unable to do what comes so easily to us, or we are unable to do what comes easily to them. This can lead to questions about ability or caring. Type development helps us make allowances for each other.

Turning now to the practicalities, how does type development take place? First, type development seems to be age-related, though not age-determined. Jung and others suggest that if our natural preferences are valued and we are supported, even as we make the inevitable mistakes, we learn to trust and value ourselves. Often, by young adulthood, we have established a working command of our dominant and auxiliary functions, and with those as a base we can use life's experience to continue our development. Second, we can consciously engage in activities which "stretch" those functions that we use less easily. It is best, at least initially, to do this under circumstances that are playful or non-demanding. This is especially true if we want to discover the joys of our fourth function. The following are examples of the conscious use and development of a less preferred function.

## Developing Sensing

If we need to develop our Sensing perceptions, it is important to focus consciously on the present moment. An example of this could be to take a walk through a park or woodland and attempt to observe the surroundings rather than the inner intuitive messages. We can notice the colors, the weather, the sounds and smells. It may be of benefit to walk in the same area in different seasons noting the changing landscape, watching a special tree come into leaf. Similarly, when undertaking a task such as preparing a meal, we can focus on the texture and essence of the ingredients rather than engaging in unrelated mental activities, however enticing they may be!

In a work setting, we may recognize certain tasks as having a sensory component – writing a detailed report or assuring accuracy in quantitative charts, for example. A care manager, with Sensing as the fourth function, describes the conscious approach to this exercise in the case study below.

> When working on a report, I come into work before my colleagues arrive because, as an Extravert, I am easily drawn into conversation with others. I close my door and settle down with a cup of coffee and my notes; I read them through and draft the document. Somehow, because my energy is high in the morning, it is quite easy. I only do one report at a time because first of all I get tired of them easily and then I start to make mistakes. I check it over later, and if it is particularly important, I go over it with a colleague. Actually, because I do it this way I enjoy it and feel the satisfaction of being able to do something like that well.

This manager describes the conscious use of the fourth function very clearly and illustrates the satisfaction that can be achieved through this process.

## Developing Intuition

If we need to develop our Intuitive perceptions, we can do so by consciously noting the hunches that come our way. People who tend to focus on Sensing describe their usual response to hunches by saying that they generally dismiss them. The hunch can instead be identified consciously, possibly discussed with someone else and even tested out.

In a work situation, Intuition can be developed by consciously looking for a number of different ways of dealing with the same problem. Those with Sensing preferences generally opt for a method that was previously found to be practical. It may assist to write down as many options as possible, however bizarre they seem! In addition, it can help to look for connections between one idea and another, to see if there is a theme running through. As an example, a pharmacist who has Intuition as a fourth function describes how he dealt with a problem in the following case study.

We had been having difficulty with providing an adequate professional service for our customers. We were taking too long to dispense their medicines. I had tried all the usual ways of tackling this problem, ensuring that the dispensing and checking procedures were working smoothly. Then I decided to look at the whole process, from the storage of our supplies, through the different use of staff, possibly altering hours to reflect our busy periods. I found it really interesting; suddenly I was seeing a wider picture of the process. I learned a lot about the ways in which we operate. We have tended to keep on working the same way without ever reviewing the whole thing. In fact, we made changes in a number of areas and they were nearly all helpful. Once I saw this, I was able to look afresh at problems in other areas of the business.

What the pharmacist discovered was his ability to widen his perspective and that, once he did so in one area, it gave him confidence to take that approach elsewhere.

## Developing Thinking

If we need to develop our Thinking judgment, we can consciously do so by identifying a decision that we have to make and trying to look at it as an outsider. The outsider will not know the personalities of the people involved, only the facts of the situation. This will focus the mind on the objective process rather than the human values involved.

In a work situation, Thinking can be developed in a similar way. When a decision has to be made, we can look first at the objective facts of the matter rather than immediately considering the personal dimension.

For example, in the case study below, a senior nurse found herself in difficulties when designing a duty list for her staff.

I found that people were always asking me for special consideration, "I need to take Sunday off because . . ." They asked me in person, sent me little notes or left telephone messages.

> I would be halfway through the job and I'd get another request. My colleagues told me I was "a soft touch." I thought about it for a long time as it took me longer and longer to complete the task. In the end I listed all the problems I had had over the last month, the number of requests I had had and those that came late. I estimated how long the job took me and compared it with my colleagues. I gave this information to my staff, asked for their input and said that, in future, the duty list would be drawn up a month in advance. After that time, only emergency changes would be considered. It really worked quite well and I felt more in control of the situation. Before I had been resentful. In addition, it was better for the staff because they could plan ahead.

The nurse discovered that, by being more objective in her approach, the task was easier and there were advantages in the new system for both herself and the staff.

## Developing Feeling

If we need to develop our Feeling judgment, we can consciously do so when we make a decision that involves people. The nurse in the last example was learning how to focus on the objective issues in her tasks. Anyone wishing to develop their Feeling function needs to work from the opposite perspective, by first considering the potential impact on people. In order to achieve this, we need to consider each problem from the perspective of each person involved. What is it like to be in their shoes?

In a work situation, Feeling can be developed when decisions have to be made that involve people. Instead of independently looking at the facts, those with a preference for Thinking can use the logic of increased involvement and diversity of perspective that will set the basis for workable decisions and full commitment. In order to achieve this it is important to identify all the people who are involved in the issue and then consider how to structure ways for viewpoints to be considered, remembering that it is the individual's subjective experience of being truly heard that matters. This is illustrated in the example below.

I am a nurse manager and I run a clinic that deals with patients who have had a heart attack. Our job is to monitor their progress and provide dietary and other advice plus supervised exercise for them. This is an area of rehabilitation that is growing in importance and one that attracts a lot of new information. We also need to implement new procedures and equipment for checking vital signs. I often find staff resistant to adopting new procedures, especially if this involves asking more of the patients. In the past, I have ensured that everyone receives information, either verbally or in writing, when practices are due to be modified. To my surprise, I found that some did not follow instructions. Next time we needed to make a change I decided that, as an experiment, I would talk to each of the six team members individually to see how it might affect them. I found that they appreciated being consulted and one said that she found it important to feel confident working with a new exercise protocol herself, before involving a patient. After that, each time we made a change we tried it out as a group and discussed it fully. It worked much better that way.

The nurse discovered that, by considering the people issues, she and the staff were able to implement better decisions.

In each of the examples we have seen that, by consciously using a different function, the people involved achieved a significant improvement in their work area. Because we tend to gravitate to our strengths, we are likely to develop blindspots. Type development, therefore, is advantageous both to us as individuals and to those with whom we work.

## Type development and the unconscious component

We have been discussing a conscious approach to type development. Many people who work with the MBTI believe that there is also an unconscious element in type development. As previously mentioned, it is felt that young people, as they build their lives, tend primarily to use their dominant and auxiliary functions. They may be even more restricted, relying heavily on the dominant alone. As we approach mid-life, however, it appears that the third and fourth functions begin to emerge. Jung (1977) remarks that the task of the first half of life is to specialize – that is, to learn to comfortably use one's dominant and auxiliary functions together with adequate use and appreciation of the third and fourth functions. During the second half of life one moves toward becoming a generalist. It is during this time that the third and fourth functions become more interesting. Their use is often seen in non-vocational areas or in a broadening of interests. From a psychological perspective the third and fourth functions are said to be closer to the unconscious, and deeper learning about the self can occur. In workshops, people can describe this process with great poignancy together with a degree of uncertainty, "this feels really weird." A good example of this was provided by Fitzgerald:

> At a leadership development program, an ESTJ (United States) military officer heard about my interest in midlife and cautiously raised the topic with me. When I described the midlife process and its possible signs, he confessed, "I can't sing the 'Star-Spangled Banner' any more." Whenever he started to sing the national anthem, he got choked up and started to cry – a reaction that greatly embarrassed him but which also showed how much he cared about what the song represented for him.
>
> (Fitzgerald 1997)

This man illustrates clearly how our less preferred functions can show up in mid-life, or, as Fitzgerald describes it, as we notice "taps on the shoulder." There is, of course, a choice as to whether the signals receive our attention or not. It is important to reinforce the fact that by attending to these signals and beginning to exercise these less preferred functions, we do not lose the facility with which we use our dominant and auxiliary functions. Different types will, not surprisingly, develop in different ways at this time and can find it difficult:

> People often experience the emergence of the tertiary [third] and inferior [fourth] functions as a combination confusing, painful, exciting, tiring, interesting and disorientating.
>
> (Fitzgerald 1997)

From this description, we can see that developing our less preferred functions can be both challenging and rewarding. It is important to appreciate this process for two reasons. First, as we have already discussed, it is important for people working in health care to understand their own preferences and to be able to access each function to a reasonable degree. Second, patients and their families may be undergoing a similar process, reacting in confusing or surprising ways as they experience the "tap on the shoulder."

## Type preference under stress

Understanding how people with different type preferences react under stress builds on the previous section since it relates again to our use of the functions. In general, when we find ourselves under pressure we tend in many ways to become "more like ourselves." We unconsciously increase our use of those skills that we trust the most. The same is true for type under stress:

- Extraverts use their dominant function in increasingly extraverted ways, saying the same thing, but this time louder, or over-repeatedly.
- Introverts use their dominant function in increasingly introverted ways, becoming quieter or more withdrawn.

This can lead to problems in interpreting each other's behavior. Introverts may have little sympathy for or understanding of the noisier Extravert, "He is always complaining, lately he talks so much and he's so loud, I can't hear myself think. I try to escape his company when he's like this." Extraverts may shrug off the perceived discomfort of the Introvert, "She never tells me anything at the best of times, now she has retreated into her shell completely, so how can I help?"

The same is true for the functions. Under stress, those with a dominant Sensing preference may become focused on each detail, while those with a dominant Intuitive function may appear to be out of touch with everyday reality. Those with a dominant Thinking preference may become extremely critical and impersonal, while those with a dominant Feeling function may become more focused on the value issues inherent in the situation. In terms of Judging and Perceiving, those preferring Judging may be obsessed with structure and completion, while Perceiving types can become lost in a mass of information while resisting structure.

## Extreme stress

In the case of extreme stress there is, once again, a considerable difference in the ways in which type preferences can be observed to react. Very occasionally, we suffer prolonged tension or a period of extreme stress. From a type standpoint what tends to happen is that in the initial stages of the situation we turn to our preferred functions, as described above. At some point, however, we can "flip" into a negative version of our fourth function, which, as already mentioned, is also referred to as the "inferior" function. Some refer to this as being in the "grip" of one's inferior function. This flip can be due to a number of factors including fatigue, acute anxiety, over-use of alcohol or drugs, or serious or long-term illness.

The resulting behavior is similar to that described by Robin Skynner and John Cleese in their book *Families and How to Survive Them* (1983). Skynner describes a metaphorical "screen" behind which individuals place and hide their unwanted characteristics. Under stress the elements and contents that have been placed behind the screen tend to spill out.

Just as the disowned behavior can tumble out uninvited from behind the screen, so the least preferred function can spring unexpectedly and powerfully into action. When this happens the function concerned is both very powerful and, at the same time, poorly developed. It is less sophisticated than those preferences we use more easily. The forceful presence of the inferior function tends to be seen in behavior that is both exaggerated and uncharacteristic. Naomi Quenk, a licensed psychologist with particular experience in researching and working in this area, describes this behavior as being "extreme . . . like a caricature of that type . . . immature . . . childish, touchy . . . undifferentiated or categorical . . . judgements will be black-and-white, all-or-none" (Quenk 1996). Often family members, colleagues or friends will describe a person who is "in the grip" as being totally unlike themselves. We may reflect on our own behavior, and say "I was just beside myself," with some chagrin.

In terms of health care, an understanding of "grip" experiences clearly has a particular relevance since patients and their families and close friends are often under particular stress. In addition, health care workers themselves can experience strain because of the nature of their job. It is equally possible that health care workers will also have problems relating to their own lives which can affect their work. A nurse whom we interviewed explained this predicament:

> I guess sensitivity to the patient is most important. Sometimes it is difficult to maintain tolerance over many years and, when my tolerance is lowered by events in my own life, I feel guilty if my sensitivity is lowered.

Table 7.2 describes examples of the ways in which the inferior function can manifest itself for different types. For reference the table

*Table 7.2* Behaviors typically expressed in "grip" situations*

| Function | Function when used as dominant | Function experienced "in the grip" |
|---|---|---|
| Sensing | • focuses on facts<br>• takes pleasure in the natural world<br><br>*In a health care setting a client may:*<br>• want to know the relevant facts and details of the illness | • beset by possibly irrelevant facts and details<br>• may become either over-identified with sensory experiences or withdrawn<br><br>*In a health care setting a client may:*<br>• be obsessed with the facts of their situation and demand or recount very detailed information, not necessarily accurately |
| Intuition | • feels at home with possibilities rather than facts<br>• interested in the future outlook or plans<br><br>*In a health care setting a client may:*<br>• ask for general long-range information about their condition | • feels out of control and may become impulsive<br>• imagines dreadful possibilities<br><br>*In a health care setting a client may:*<br>• imagine the worst possible scenarios and make rash decisions about their treatment |
| Thinking | • tends to be logical and non personal<br>• focuses on competence which may include objective criticism<br><br>*In a health care setting a client may:*<br>• ask for clear, truthful information and make objective decisions<br>• notice and comment on what isn't working well, intending to be helpful | • may be convinced that a twisted logic is indeed accurate, resulting in hasty or reckless behavior<br>• aggressively critical<br><br>*In a health care setting a client may:*<br>• become judgmental or strike out verbally |

(*continues*)

*Table 7.2    (continued)*

| Function | Function when used as dominant | Function experienced "in the grip" |
|---|---|---|
| Feeling | • primarily interested in human values and harmony<br>• interested in forming relationships or a personal communication<br><br>*In a health care setting a client may*:<br>• seek personal attention and acceptance before requesting clinical information<br>• want to be known to a person before sharing or requesting clinical information | • may become over-anxious and uncontrollably emotional<br>• loses a sense of self-worth<br><br>*In a health care setting a client may*:<br>• become suddenly overwhelmed by emotion and fear<br>• lose sense of being able to handle the situation |

*Adapted from FLEX Care® by Susan A. Brock, 1999. Reprinted with permission.

also contains a summary of the same function when used effectively in its dominant form.

A full discussion of the inferior function is beyond the scope of this book. We would suggest you read *Beside Ourselves* (Quenk 1993) and *In the Grip* (Quenk 1996) for a more complete treatment. Our purpose here is to alert health care professionals to this important source of insight connected to type preference. This aspect of type theory can help to explain reactions in oneself and others that were not only unpleasant but baffling.

Whatever the functional preferences of the individual experiencing this uncomfortable "grip" situation, a number of practical questions arise.

### How will we know when someone is in the "grip?"

The person, as previously mentioned, will be behaving in a way that seems very out of character. For example, a patient who is usually logical may become extremely emotional and tearful. Relatives may report that the patient has been acting unusually. They themselves may be distressed by this. On the other hand, "type isn't everything." If the behavior continues or deepens consider other aetiologies such as drug reactions or other clinical manifestations.

### What can we do about it?

Throughout the book, we have referred to the importance of mirroring functional preferences. This is one time when that is not appropriate. We need to provide a sense of security for the patient, an indication that we are aware of the degree of distress they are undergoing and that we are there to help when and if they desire it. Knowing about this aspect of behavior can help us to be more tolerant. Using type-based phrases, such as "you seem to be having a 'grip' experience," will definitely not be welcome. Empathy may be the best solution, "You say that you have had more serious pain over the last few days and that it is making you feel incredibly depressed." It may help the patient to regain their balance if the initial problem, the pain, is addressed immediately and the patient *knows* that something is happening.

### Does an understanding of type theory prevent "grip" experiences from happening?

In a word, "No." Despite an understanding of type, "grip" experiences will continue to occur. However, understanding type theory, insight into the process and taking time to develop the less favored functions may reduce the frequency and severity of "grip" experiences.

### Do we benefit in any way from having "grip" experiences?

"Grip" experiences tend to occur when our lives are out of balance. They can act as a signal to help us to regain our equilibrium:

> The inferior function is a natural teacher that reminds you when your energies are depleted, shows you new avenues for development.
> (Pearman and Albritton 1997)

### How do we return to balance?

There is no specific recipe for returning to balance, simply because there are numerous variations and degrees within the experience. We have asked individuals with different type preferences to explain what is important for them in this situation.

### Dominant Sensing – inferior Intuition
### (ISTP, ESTP, ISTJ, ISFJ)

When I become overwhelmed by facts, I need help to provide a framework. This doesn't mean I want to be told what to do, nor do I want someone to trivialize or minimize the problems. When I'm under pressure I can see the problems but I lose the ability to see the overall situation. I need to be reminded of those things I have done well in the past, some practical achievement, because I imagine all the things that could go wrong in the future. I can really obsess about negative possibilities.

Once this happened when I had been running a department without an important member of staff for six months. I was tired out. What I needed most was practical help and understanding of my situation. I actually wanted someone to solve the problem for me or show me how to do so. It only resolved when the person concerned – who had been on sick leave – decided to leave and we found a replacement.

### Dominant Intuition – inferior Sensing
### (ENTP, ENFP, INTJ, INFJ)

When I become obsessed with facts, I find people don't accept what I say, they simply think I am complaining or being ridiculous. When I discovered that a trusted colleague had been involved in stealing drugs from our department, I found myself intent on finding every last shred of evidence. The thing was, I had known at the back of my mind that there was a problem and talked to the managers but no one believed me. It would have helped me most if I had been listened to but the extreme way I was going about it made it difficult for others to do that. I became completely exhausted and actually ill and did not begin to feel better until a security check proved me right. More than anything it helped me when my concerns were taken seriously.

## Dominant Thinking – inferior Feeling
## (ESTJ, ENTJ, ISTP, INTP)

What I don't want is someone to say "I know how that feels" because they don't. I need someone that I trust and who genuinely understands and has something to offer. Because I feel helpless in the situation, I need to do something small to feel that I am doing something. It's a bit like constructing a ladder so that I can climb out of the pit. I worked for a long period in a job that didn't suit me, I got more and more stressed until I flipped. It was so out of character I scared even myself. Finally, I talked to a trusted friend who listened to me and didn't keep saying things like, "but it's such a good job, you'd be crazy to leave." The only real solution was to move, so I did. It proved to be a good decision.

## Dominant Feeling – inferior Thinking
## (ESFJ, ENFJ, ISFP, INFP)

What is most important for me is that other people don't keep explaining the logical course of action, or pointing out past errors of judgment – often that was part of the problem in the first place. I am a nurse and I work in a management team where I am called the "people person." Sometimes I feel that this is used as a "put down." I got particularly angry with one of the human resource managers, she just saw nurses as numbers and we had an especially bad disagreement over staffing levels in a clinic. Afterwards, I couldn't stop thinking about what an awful person she was. I found it helpful when a close colleague listened to my distress, appeared to understand my point of view and spoke to her for me. This gave me a much-needed space.

Despite different ways of expressing the experience of returning to balance, each one of the people above asks to have their situation taken seriously, not to be patronized or to have their situation rationalized. In many ways, this reflects the theme of this book, which is carried on into the next chapter when we introduce the Mobius Model and the concept of conversations for mutual understanding. In each situation we have described, the essence of communication is being able to focus on the needs of the other, even when they differ substantially from our own.

## Exercise

1  Find your type preference in Table 7.1. How has your type development proceeded? Were your dominant and auxiliary functions encouraged during your adolescence and early adulthood? What circumstances have encouraged the development of your third and fourth functions?
2  What things come easily to you? What comes with more difficulty? Do these things reflect your third and fourth functions?
3  Think of an example in your working life where you consciously use your less preferred functions successfully. What helped you to do this? Note how you felt.
4  Recall an instance when you were in the grip of your inferior (fourth) function. What caused it and how did you begin to return to balance?
5  Think of one or two learning points about type development, handling stress/extreme stress, or recognizing a "grip" experience, which could help you in your personal and professional life.

## Summary

In this chapter we have examined how an understanding of type dynamics can lead to a deeper understanding of self, others and interaction. For any given type the term *preference* comes to life in a more meaningful way. We truly prefer and use our dominant preference as a "first stop," but we can and do factor in our less preferred functions. An awareness of those less preferred functions helps us choose developmental strategies and provides a bridge to valuing others. Possibly of even greater value is understanding the role our personal type dynamics plays during normal stress. Stressors are not likely to go away but a perspective on how and why we and others react as we do increases our acceptance and tolerance – in itself helping to lower stress!

# 8 Creating committed action

This chapter will introduce a model which is independent of the MBTI but which has important links with it. The framework, called the Mobius Model©, describes how to create conversations that result in dialogue and committed action. Type adds an important perspective onto that framework. In this chapter, the relationship of the Mobius Model and the MBTI material will be explored.

## Background

A Möbius strip is a figure that appears to have two surfaces but actually has only one (see Figure 8.1). A three-dimensional representation can be made by taking a strip of paper, twisting it over once and then attaching the two ends. The result resembles a figure "8" or the infinity sign. If a finger, or a pencil, is run along the surface of the model it will trace a continuous line on all surfaces and will return to its starting place, never having been removed from the surface. The Möbius strip was adopted by Bill Stockton as a symbol for communication because each of us actually has two conversations going on simultaneously. One is the outer conversation heard by others. The other is one's inner conversation, which plays in our head. When we engage in conversations with others that result in real dialogue and create committed action, our own two conversations, the inner and the outer, are congruent. We are able to say what we are thinking in a straightforward and respectful way. These conversations are literally creative, providing understanding, empathy, new ideas and perspective.

They can form an integral part of daily life and are, of course, particularly important and sensitive when people become seriously ill. The Mobius Model can be a roadmap showing how to create conversations that aid the caring process. We will see that type

*Figure 8.1* The Möbius strip

elements are analogous to the various vehicles to be used on that road.

Bill Stockton developed the Mobius Model following many years' experience as a cultural anthropologist and organizational development consultant. He realized that his work involved, almost exclusively, conversations with other people. He further recognized that not all such exchanges were creative. That is, many conversations were simply reruns of prior conversations, often blaming and certainly not moving a situation toward resolution or opening up a new perspective. The Mobius Model has been developed over a period of more than ten years in an attempt to identify and transform uncreative communications into ones that create new perspective, mutual understanding and committed action. A major key to creating conversations that are congruent is to actively work towards mutual understanding. This involves the behaviors of active listening, often talked about in patient care. Careful attention to "listening for understanding," not listening for "agree or disagree," is central.

## THE MOBIUS MODEL

What are the steps or sequence of communication that lead to this state of integrated communication?

The Mobius Model, illustrated in Figure 8.2, is divided into six sections. The section at the top which is labeled "Well-being" or "mutual understanding" provides the preferred entry point into the continuous process. In creative exchanges, the conversation develops

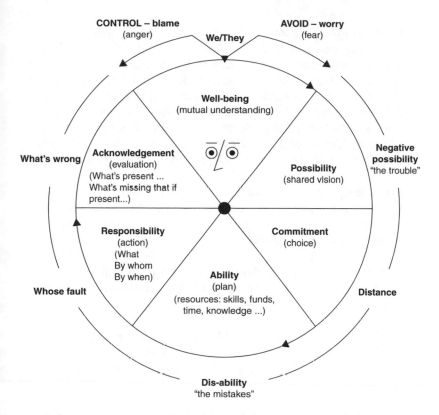

*Figure 8.2* The Mobius Model©: Creating Committed Action (The Mobius Model, 1984, Bill Stockton, Creative Conversations, Inc. Adapted with permission by Susan A. Brock from FLEX Talk®, 1991 Brock Associates, Minneapolis, MN)

from this starting point in a clockwise direction, as can be seen in the following example.

---

Mrs Giles has been seeing her local cancer care nurse for six months. Recently she went to stay with her daughter for three weeks, having received a grant for the train fare. She has returned and her oncology nurse telephones her to arrange a visit. An outline of the conversation follows.

**Well-being** – is established; the nurse asks how the visit went and hears that Mrs Giles enjoyed it all very much although she found it tiring. Questions concerning her health received generally positive replies but again Mrs Giles said she was tired. The nurse was not listening to correct, or hear only what went well – or indeed to provide instant solutions. She was listening for understanding. She was taking in the whole of Mrs Giles's experience and truly accepting it. This establishes a sense of trust and builds a foundation for rapport.

**Possibility** – having established rapport, the nurse suggests that they meet that week and discuss possible causes for the tiredness. The nurse suggests this as a possibility, and is open to other possibilities.

**Commitment** – on reflection, Mrs Giles agrees that she would like to explore the reasons for her fatigue and states, "I'll look forward to that."

**Ability** – the nurse reminds Mrs Giles of the Friday Club at the Health Center and asks if it is convenient for them to meet there. Mrs Giles agrees but says she will need transportation.

**Responsibility** – the nurse confirms that she will arrange for transportation and they agree on a time for Mrs Giles to be ready.

**Acknowledgement** – Mrs Giles thanks the nurse for ringing and says she is grateful not to have been forgotten while she was away. The conversation has set a mode of communication that allows Mrs Giles and the nurse to express both their inner conversation and the more socially acceptable outer conversation. An expectation for "real" conversation has been set. This will allow for important issues and feelings to be discussed as they occur.

This example is purposely straightforward and illustrates how creative conversations can be mapped onto the Mobius Model. The next example, based on a similar situation, illustrates the development of an uncreative exchange. For this example, there is a complicating factor not known to the nurse: Mrs Giles's departure for her family visit was delayed because a prescription that the nurse had told her would be ready at the clinic, was not. The receptionist said that it had not been ordered. Mrs Giles finally got the prescription but it was incomplete and she had had to see a doctor while she was away in order to obtain supplies. Her son-in-law had told her that she was not receiving sufficient attention and should ask for home visits in the future.

**Well-being** – when the nurse rang and asked about her vacation, Mrs Giles replied that it had been all right but "no thanks to you." She was clearly angry and was tending to blame.

From here, the conversation can be followed on Figure 8.2 in a counter-clockwise direction.

**Acknowledgement ("What's wrong?")** – the nurse asked what was wrong and Mrs Giles told her she had had to be preoccupied with her medical needs instead of having a real break. Mrs Giles ended with, "you didn't order my medicines and you promised me you would." The "what's wrong" step on the outer circle can lead to real understanding and acknowledgement of the situation. If this step is followed with listening for understanding, well-being can be created and the conversation can turn into a clockwise, creative exchange. It is, however, very tempting to move unconsciously in the counter-clockwise direction, as illustrated next.

**Responsibility ("Whose fault?")** – the nurse replied that she had requested the prescription and had asked for an extra supply ". . . it isn't my fault, it must have been lost at the clinic. . . ." A counter-clockwise responsibility conversation often has an underlying issue of "whose fault?"

**Ability (Dis-ability)** – Mrs Giles replied that "they were always making mistakes but she had trusted her nurse, until now." She is verbally placing the nurse in the position of "they" who don't *really* care and can't be trusted. She went on to say ". . . and my son-in-law says I am not getting the attention I should, he thinks I should have home visits all the time, not keep coming to the clinic."

**Commitment (Distancing)** – the nurse does not use active listening skills to let Mrs Giles know that her distress has been heard and appreciated. When the nurse perseveres to try to get the patient to take a desired action by asking if she would come to the Friday Club, Mrs Giles replies "no." (Some patients would have said "yes," just to go along with her, then not have shown up.)

**Possibility (Trouble)** – "If I want you to call again, which is unlikely, I'll ring but I will expect you to come here." The nurse thinks, "My word, here I am trying to help and I simply receive abuse." Although the nurse knows that Mrs Giles feels bad physically and emotionally, she begins to see Mrs Giles as "one of those patients you can never please." Both have withdrawn to stances which maintain that further communication will only lead to more trouble.

**Well-being – mutual understanding (We–They)** – both Mrs Giles and the nurse begin to hold an opinion about the other that further separates them from each other. "Those doctors and nurses just call at their own convenience." "These patients can be so difficult, even when I go out of my way." Both individuals are likely to express their opinion to several other individuals inviting others into the counter-clockwise spin of "we–they" and "blame."

This example illustrates the distinctly different routes a conversation can take and how hard it can be to break the cycle and return to a creative exchange.

Neither is reporting and receiving the internal conversations of disappointment and frustration. They have both moved into a we–they stance that can make it even easier to mis-communicate in the future.

## Blame and worry monologues

The outer circle of the Mobius Model represents two kinds of monologue which take place when people feel misunderstood or let down in some way. These monologues are conversations in which individuals can appear to be sharing points of view. In reality no true sharing of meaning, that is dialogue, is taking place. Instead, an individual is expressing a point of view, wanting very much to be understood, only to have that point of view countered by the other individual who also is intent on being understood rather than understanding.

### The blame cycle

As you read this list, you will see how Mrs Giles goes step by step through the situation, each step building on the one before. The words added in italics can be followed from Figure 8.2.

* I had to be preoccupied with medical needs instead of being free to relax – *what's wrong*
* The prescription wasn't there – *what's wrong*
* It must be someone's fault, the nurse's – *whose fault*
* They always make mistakes – *dis-ability*
* I don't want to come to the Friday Club, I want to keep my distance or at least maintain control – *distance*
* I will insist you come to me, I don't want to be forgotten again – *trouble, negative possibilities*
* You're like all the health service, not really interested or understanding – just one more "they" that has to be fought to receive care – *me/they*

Meanwhile, the nurse may be on the outer clockwise "worry cycle."

### The worry cycle

The nurse is working through the same situation but in her head, which means that Mrs Giles is unaware of it. Again, the step-by-step process unfolds, moving deeper into trouble.

* This could cause trouble (for me with the clinic and Mrs Giles) – *trouble, negative possibilities*
* I don't want to fall out with Mrs Giles (maybe I'll just back off and let her cool down) – *distance*
* Could I have forgotten to order her prescription for her? – *dis-ability*
* It must have been the clinic's fault, and her son-in-law certainly doesn't help either – *whose fault*
* This is a mess. I just want to be rid of it – *what's wrong*
* Maybe I should find a less stressful position. I don't think I'm up to what "they" need – *me/they*

Equally, the nurse may also have moved into a blaming monologue by immediately implicating the clinic, "they always let me down."

*Establishing dialogue*

At the top of the Mobius Model in Figure 8.2 a diagrammatic arrow-shaped triangle entry point can be seen. A triangle is the symbol for change. In this position, it highlights a route into creative dialogue. This is where the potential power of the model becomes apparent. Mrs Giles and her nurse are spinning around the outer circle. How can they resolve their difficulties and re-establish their relationship?

*Well-being*

In order to enter the inner circle and move clockwise, the nurse needs to understand the problem from Mrs Giles's point of view. This is fundamentally different from agreeing with her. Often, for any helping professional, distinguishing between listening to agree and listening to understand is the key to their facilitative role. Using the counseling technique of active listening and reflecting back, the nurse could have asked Mrs Giles to tell her what happened. This is an invitation to share her "what's wrong" story. At the appropriate intervals this might include:

> so you went to the surgery . . . the prescription wasn't ready and they said it hadn't been ordered . . . you had to wait for the doctor to sign one and you nearly missed the train . . . you were particularly worried because you had a seat booked and your daughter was meeting you.

Knowledge of the Mobius "blame" pattern can help the professional maintain a stance of listening for understanding instead of being sucked into the blame or worry mode. The conversation for understanding would include the comments made by her son-in-law drawn out in the same way. This may well be difficult, particularly since the nurse clearly helped with the preparations for the trip (by ordering the medicines) and may feel seriously aggrieved – hence the temptation to blame or worry. Once into her story, and sure she was being "heard," Mrs Giles may allow more problems to emerge, "I felt I was a burden, my daughter is so busy . . . he was annoyed when we had to go to the clinic."

Eventually, however annoyed she may have been, Mrs Giles will know that the nurse understands what happened and is seeing it from her point of view. In Figure 8.2 there are two eyes which symbolize "my eye and your eye" looking at the problem. It is the act of looking at the problem from slightly different but co-ordinated perspectives that facilitates finding new possibilities. This is much like our two eyes providing binocular vision that results in depth perception – a wholly different way of seeing.

Only when Mrs Giles has told all her story and feels that the nurse understands will she be willing – in any meaningful sense – to move forward and consider possibilities. It is important to emphasize that possibilities are not the same as solutions. This is a difficult concept especially for nurses or other health care professionals who tend to see themselves in the role of solving problems. A tempting solution might be, "I'll go to the clinic to check (to prove me right)," or "maybe I'd better not visit the family for a while. . . ." It is also important to realize that *real* possibilities, that is, those that can be fully entertained or accepted, will not occur unless a sense of well-being (mutual understanding) is present first.

Mrs Giles has been invited to say what she sees as wrong. She has been heard. The nurse has listened to understand. She has maintained a stance of non-defensiveness because she is not concerned with who is right or wrong. The Mobius Model framework has helped her to understand and track the conversation. At this point, the nurse may be able to turn the conversation into the inner circle.

### Acknowledgement

One question that often helps to turn a conversation is a version of "What's missing for you that, if it *were* present, would move you/us to the desired goal?" Sometimes it actually helps to list the "What's wrongs," then ask the "What's missing that if it were present" question.

For example, the "What's wrong" list might include:

- My prescription wasn't ready.
- It spoiled the start of my visit.
- I ran out of tablets.
- My son-in-law was cross.
- He criticized my local care.
- My daughter was short with me.

The list would continue to grow until she felt it contained everything of note.

*What's missing that, if it were present, you'd feel
supported?*

This part of the exercise is the most demanding. At first sight "what's
missing?" may be seen as simply the opposite of "what's wrong?"
Those experienced in the use of this model find that it is the "if it
were present" column that ultimately provides the key to the problem,
or, to put it another way, it gives a clearer focus on the nature of
the issue, new possibilities emerge.

The corresponding lists might look like this:

| What's wrong? | What's missing that if it *were* present? |
|---|---|
| 1  My prescription wasn't ready | Correct medicines for my trip. Trust in the nurse and the clinic. Knowing that they care |
| 2  It spoiled the start of my vacation | The happy memory of the visit I'd hoped to have |
| 3  I ran out of tablets | Enough correct medicines so I didn't need to be a trouble to my daughter and son-in-law. This maintains the belief my daughter had that I could cope |
| 4  My son-in-law was cross | Our usual easy-going relationship. He has always said I'm "no bother" |
| 5  He criticized my local care | I thought the set-up at home was great, now I've lost my nerve a bit |
| 6  My daughter was short with me | The feeling that they liked to see me. I want to be helpful and needed, not a bother |

This example demonstrates the depth of information that might have
been missed if the nurse had not addressed the matter by listening
and creating real understanding. Working through it may also have
highlighted hidden anxieties for Mrs Giles herself – the issues that
she found hard to identify and confront.

Mrs Giles and her nurse can now begin to address commitment,
the next phase in the model. They can look at the issues raised and
decide which she wishes to take forward, and which she would rather

leave, for the present at least. From there they can progress to putting a plan in place, clarifying responsibilities and setting a check-back time to acknowledge "What's now present" and "What, if anything, is now missing that if it were present would support you."

The temptation when presented with the list of "What's wrong?" – again, especially for nurses and carers – is to put it right with quick assurances. In the case of Mrs Giles this might have included:

- I'll go and sort things out at the surgery.
- Even though it was difficult, I'm sure your trip made up for it.
- I'm sure your daughter knows you can manage, I expect they're just worried about you.
- You don't need to worry, I'll take care of you . . . we all deserve to be waited on as we grow older . . . and that's what *I'm* here for.

Health professionals working in Mobius Model workshops find it both tempting and frustrating to use "the Band-Aid" approach. The objective is clarity and insight, not reactive solutions or reassurances. The former tend to be short-term, the latter, long-term. One reinforces the status quo, the other provides scope for the development of patient independence and a helping relationship.

### The team context

The Mobius Model can be applied in exactly the same way to a problem between colleagues. One example of this is contained in the following brief case history.

The "trouble story" conversation took place in a situation in which a doctor continually found difficulty in gaining the respect and friendship of her colleagues. Her "What's wrong?" list was full of phrases such as "my partner does not respect me, my employees do not carry out my wishes, I am always being interrupted by receptionists." Arriving at the relevant "What's missing?" column, she could not see the answer. Gently assisted she realized that the key word was "communication." This helped her to begin to look at *her* responsibility in this area and to begin to see that unless she made her wishes clear it was not possible for anyone to meet her requirements.

The doctor began to realize that she had been in the blame mode, seeking to discover who was responsible for her difficulties. She took the MBTI and discovered she had preferences for Introversion and Feeling. She began to see that she preferred to work in a quiet atmosphere and that she found asserting her own needs to be very difficult. Talking it over, it became clear to her that the reception-ists needed contact with her but that this could be arranged at a mutually convenient time. As she talked, she looked at the Mobius Model (Figure 8.2) and traced her finger from the words "worry" and "blame" towards "mutual understanding." She said, "I am begin-ning to see that communication is two-way, and the more I avoid it, the more people try to make me do it. I can see that for real communication to happen I need to express my point of view and let others know I hear and understand their point of view." From this point she was able to begin to enter the clockwise Mobius circle, starting with thinking about possible steps she could take toward working creatively with her problem rather than blaming others.

## The Mobius Model and type

Stockton has worked together with Brock, looking at links between the Mobius Model and the MBTI.

Their first hypothesis is that, in terms of the monologues described on the outer circle it is likely that those with a preference for Extraversion, energized by the outer world, will be drawn initially to "blame." Those with a preference for the inner world of Introversion may initially "worry." This clearly reflects the "Talk it Out" and "Think it Through" preferences described in the Four-Part Framework (Brock 1992, revised from 1987). Health professionals working with the Mobius Model agree that this may not always be the case but, as with type preferences, there may well be a predictable preference.

**Well-being** is seen as being the province of the Feeling function, promoting interpersonal understanding. Those with the logical Thinking preference may be prone to skipping, or moving quickly past, this part of an interaction, "now ... to the business!"

**Possibility** provides a magnetic pull for those who prefer Intuition, the "Big Picture" people, who like alternatives and options. They might stick in this section playing with possibilities and options, leav-ing others mystified as to "what's the purpose here?" or wishing they had more specific facts to work with – and quite possibly irritated.

**Commitment** – this is an area that is more complicated due to the dynamics of type. At the most immediate level, it seems reason-able to assume that commitment may be a quicker process for those with a Judging preference. The Mobius Model provides a reminder that commitment is only part of the process. And more importantly, it is a product built on the work completed together in the previous phases, of "Well-being" and "Possibilities."

**Ability** represents the development of a logical framework, the strength of the Thinking function. "If" we want to achieve our commitment, "then" the logical steps should be. . . ." Setting out a plan and evaluating resources provide comfortable activities for Thinking types to accomplish the commitment. Those with a preference for Feeling may be less energized by this planning process but can be on the lookout to be sure that the plan of action matches the people-oriented values they prize.

**Responsibility** – the details of who does what and when require an eye for practical matters which is most likely to be met by the Sensing function. Again, those with a preference for Intuition may not automatically be energized by this step.

**Acknowledgement** – as with commitment, the link to type is somewhat more complex, but those with a Perceiving function are more likely to revisit the problem and check that no options have been overlooked, while those with a Judging function may quickly consider the matter to be closed and want to move on to another issue.

Again, the Mobius Model provides a roadmap for adjusting to continually changing circumstances. At the same time, type provides the "vehicles" for different parts of the road. Together, the Mobius Model and type form an important perspective both in patient care and in the team context.

It has been emphasized throughout this book that when working with type we need to remember that it is possible for each person to choose to use all the preferences, if with varying levels of skill. The importance of this perspective in relation to the Mobius Model is that those who are aware of their own type may be able to recognize the areas on which they tend to concentrate and those which they may skip.

## Clinical applications for the Mobius Model

The Mobius Model can be used to encourage positive, meaningful conversations, as the examples demonstrate. The matching of inner and outer conversations can lead to creative exchanges in the most difficult circumstances. When a knowledge of type is added, a health care professional can be aware of the pieces of dialogue they tend to either over- or under-utilize.

The following is an example of a suggested potential application followed by an exercise to put the model into practice.

### Delivering an unwelcome message

We often have to share information with patients that they will not welcome: extended treatment periods, that their blood picture has not improved as hoped – many examples come to mind. We may not look forward to the meeting and may tend to migrate more quickly than usual to the phase of the Mobius Model where we feel most at home. However, by going through each phase both parties are more likely to leave the discussion feeling satisfied.

The emphasis in each phase of the Mobius Model is:

- **Well-being**: ensuring, through active listening, that the patient feels fully involved in the discussion and is clear about what is being discussed. The essence of this is for each individual to hear and accept the perspective and information of the other. This allows for new understanding or depth perception and prepares the patient and practitioner for any necessary action.
- **Possibilities**: giving a clear picture of whatever options exist, and engaging the patient in thinking about options, the health care professional ensures that the patient is aware of their choices and helps insure later commitment.
- **Commitment**: working together so that the patient can absorb the information and commit to action. The focus here is setting the goal or direction that the patient has evaluated and chosen. The patient knows what she/he is shooting for.
- **Ability**: working with the patient to form a plan of action that will achieve the commitment. This may include the treatment plan, other outside resources, payment issues and the like.
- **Responsibility**: establishing with the patient who will make any necessary arrangements and how they will receive the information, and what specific steps the patient needs to take.
- **Acknowledgement**: providing an overview of the discussion, encouraging the patient to express any uncertainties or anxieties, making sure that she/he leaves with the relevant information, including a personal contact for further advice, preferably in writing. It is often helpful to mention that the patient's situation or needs may change along the way and that that is our expectation – and that the plan and circumstances will shift if necessary. This leads to setting up follow-up dates, telephone calls or assessments.

# Exercises

1
   (a) Think of a time when you communicated with a patient particularly well and break the conversation down under the Mobius Model headings. You may want to consider your own type preferences and identify the possible effects of those. Are you, for example, good at creating rapport, well-being (Feeling preference), or do you tend to focus first on another phase of the Mobius Model?

   (b) Now think of a situation where you felt dissatisfied with an interaction. It got stuck somewhere. Can you identify on the model where it became stuck? Did it start out as a "blame" or "worry" conversation in which there was "listening for agree/disagree?" Or was there "listening for understanding" to gain and exchange perspectives? If possible look for a link between your type preferences and the point where the communication went wrong. Did you both move to a particular "phase" then find problems later since issues had not surfaced or been discussed? What might you want to do differently another time?

2   This is a practical exercise for which you need a partner. Sit back-to-back, to avoid eye contact. Hold an imaginary telephone conversation. You can agree on the overall subject in advance but do not prepare a script. Decide who is to be the caller and who the receiver. Role-play one easy conversation. The patient might start with "what's wrong?" and the practitioner might practice "listening for understanding," moving to "what's missing that, if it were present, would help in the situation?" Afterwards, look at the model and identify the stages that were – or were not – covered in your dialogue.

# Summary

The Mobius Model can be used at different levels. It can guide personal understanding, helping a patient move from blame or worry into a dialogue that produces committed action. It can be used at the team and organizational level to recognize instances where the "outer conversation" is not congruent with the "inner conversation." A signal of this state of affairs may be when team members have a separate meeting after the official meeting to discuss what was undiscussable.

Used with type, the Mobius Model provides understanding as to why certain phases of conversations to create committed action are intriguing while others are automatic, distasteful or forgotten.

As with the MBTI and the work on developing influencing skills, the Mobius Model supplies another highly effective compass with which to navigate personal interactions.

© Mobius is a copyright of Mobius Inc., William Stockton Ph.D.

*The authors wish to thank Bill Stockton and his professional partner, Marjorie Herdes, for providing tutorial help on the Mobius Model and personal support in the preparation of this chapter.*

# 9  Next steps

The Myers-Briggs Type Indicator (MBTI) is essentially a practical model as well as a theoretical one. This final chapter contains information about going on from here to find MBTI courses and further reading. Because the MBTI is a psychological instrument, anyone administering the MBTI or conducting courses is required to hold a recognized qualification to do so. When in doubt contact Consulting Psychologists Press (USA), the publisher of the instrument, or Oxford Psychologists Press (the distributor of the instrument in the UK). We list below the details of several major organizations in the United Kingdom, Canada and the United States who provide either training or MBTI-related materials.

We suggest searching the World Wide Web using key words such as MBTI, the Myers-Briggs Type Indicator, and Psychological Type. In addition, you may want to search academic journals in your area for current research articles related to psychological type.

When reviewing books, articles or other materials take care to be a discriminating consumer. Remember there are no better or worse types. The materials should present a balanced point of view regarding all types.

## United Kingdom

**British Association of Psychological Type (BAPT)**
PO Box 48, Honiton, Devon EX14 OXY
Telephone:   01404 850267
Fax:         01404 850302
E-mail:      admin@bapt.org.uk

- Provides information regarding qualified practitioners by geographical area.

**Oxford Psychologists Press**
15–17 Elsfield Way, Oxford OX2 8EP
Telephone:   01865 510203
Fax:         01865 310368
E-mail:      orders@opp.co.uk
Web site:    www.opp.co.uk

- Provides scoring services and is a distributor for MBTI materials, books and other psychological instruments.
- Conducts qualifying courses for MBTI practitioners.
- Conducts advanced application courses for the MBTI.

## United States

**The Association for Psychological Type (APT)**
Association Management Center, 4700 W. Lake Avenue, Glenview, IL 60025
Telephone:   847 375 4717
Fax:         847 375 4777
E-mail:      staff@aptcentral.org
Web site:    www.aptcentral.org

- International membership organization for those interested in psychological type theories and applications.
- Conducts qualifying courses for MBTI practitioners.
- Conducts advanced application courses for the MBTI.
- Support local and regional chapters.

**Center for Applications of Psychological Type (CAPT)**
2815 NW 13th Street, Suite 401, Gainesville, FL 32609
Telephone:   352 375 0160
Fax:         352 378 0503
E-mail:      staff@capt.org
Web site:    www.capt.org

- Conducts qualifying courses for MBTI practitioners.
- Conducts advanced application courses for the MBTI.
- Supplies MBTI books and training materials.
- Provides research scoring services and research consultation.
- Conducts research and bibliographic searches on type-related subjects.
- Organizes conferences in specialized areas such as health, leadership and multicultural applications.

**Consulting Psychologists Press**
3803 East Bayshore Road, PO Box 10096, Palo Alto, CA 94303
Telephone: 650 969 8901
Fax: 650 969 8608
E-mail: custserv@cpp-db.com
Web site: www.cpp-db.com

- Publisher of the Myers-Briggs Type Indicator.
- Provides scoring services, books and materials on the Myers-Briggs Type Indicator and other psychological instruments.

## Canada

**Psychometrics Canada**
7125 77th Avenue, Edmonton, Alberta T6B 0B5, Canada
Telephone: 780 469 2268
Fax: 780 469 2283
E-mail: info@psychometrics.com
Web site: www.psychometrics.com

- Provides scoring services and is a distributor for MBTI materials, books and other psychological instruments.
- Conducts qualifying courses for MBTI practitioners.
- Conducts advanced application courses for the MBTI.
- Services and products available in both English and French.

## FURTHER READING

### General

*Introduction to Type* (1998)
Isabel Briggs Myers, revised by Linda K. Kirby and Katharine D. Myers
Consulting Psychologists Press
A 40-page introductory book, which contains the basic essentials of MBTI type theory. A number of course leaders provide this book for those undertaking basic MBTI courses.

*Gifts Differing* (1980)
Isabel Briggs Myers
Consulting Psychologists Press

Isabel Myers' original book describing her type theory and some applications, including type dynamics and type development.

*I'm Not Crazy, I'm Just Not You: The Real Meaning of the 16 Personality Types* (1997)
Roger R. Pearman and Sarah C. Albritton
Davies-Black Publishing
*I'm Not Crazy, I'm Just Not You* is based on extensive research carried out by the authors. The book addresses the sensitive issues of bias and discrimination by type. Although it contains considerable detail, it is suitable for readers with a limited knowledge of type.

*Journal of Psychological Type*
Thomas G. Carskadon, editor
This is a refereed journal of papers and discussions related to psychological type. Department of Psychology, Box 6161, Mississippi State University, Mississippi State, MS 39762. E-mail: tomcar@ra.msstate.edu

*The Myers-Briggs Type Indicator: A Critical Review and Practical Guide (1997)*
Rowan Bayne
Chapman and Hall
Rowan Bayne presents a critical review of MBTI research and type concepts within a practical framework. Looks particularly at applications in counseling, education and organizations.

*MBTI Manual: A Guide to the Development and Use of the Myers-Briggs Type Indicator, Third edition* (1998)
I. Briggs Myers, M.H. McCaulley, N.L. Quenk and A.L. Hammer
Consulting Psychologists Press
Newly updated manual provides a comprehensive overview of MBTI uses and applications. In addition to chapters on theory, administration and interpretation and the like, there are extensive sections on counseling and psychotherapy, use of type in education management and leadership and multicultural applications.

*LIFETypes* (1989)
S.K. Hirsh and J.M. Kummerow
Warner Books
A popular introduction to type focusing on life and work.

*Looking at Type: The Fundamentals* (1997)
Charles R. Martin
Center for Applications of Psychological Type
The book covers the basic nature of type as a dynamic model of personality, detailed descriptions of all sixteen personality types and unique paths to personal growth.

*Type Dynamics and Type Development* (1994)
Katharine D. Myers and Linda A. Kirby
Consulting Psychologists Press
This book explores type dynamics and type development and is particularly relevant for those wishing to develop their understanding of type theory.

## Applications of type theory

*Introduction to Type in Organizations* (1998)
Sandra K. Hirsh and Jean M. Kummerow
Consulting Psychologists Press
This 32-page booklet provides a basic understanding of the MBTI both on an individual basis and how type differences affect communication and team dynamics.

*The Character of Organizations* (1992)
William Bridges
Consulting Psychologists Press
William Bridges describes sixteen organizational types based upon MBTI theory, illustrating, together with examples, the ways in which type affects organizational behavior.

*In the Grip* (1996)
Naomi Quenk
Consulting Psychologists Press
*In the Grip* examines the ways in which people with different type preferences might respond to stressful situations.

*Beside Ourselves* (1993)
Naomi Quenk
Consulting Psychologists Press
Develops the issues identified in *In the Grip* in greater depth and introduces elements of Jungian theory.

*Looking at Type and Spirituality* (1997)
Sandra K. Hirsh and Jane A.G. Kise
*Center for Applications of Psychological Type*
*Looking at Type and Spirituality* explains how type preferences may affect the ways in which individuals choose to express their spirituality.

*Looking at Type in the Workplace* (1997)
Larry Demarest
Center for Applications of Psychological Type
How an individual's psychological type affects their interactions at work including responding to conflict, work style, being part of a team, making decisions, dealing with change and communication.

*Managing Transitions – Making the Most of Change* (1991)
William Bridges
Addison-Wesley
Bridges describes change by recognizing the component parts that need to be openly identified during a period of change. The book contains information about the different stages of change and provides checklists to help individuals and groups assess their progress.

*The Challenge of Change in Organizations* (1995)
Nancy J. Barger and Linda K. Kirby
Davies-Black Publishing
This book addresses the issue of why different people react differently to change. It refers to Bridges' theory of change and develops it further, including information about the links between MBTI theory and change.

*Developing Leaders: Research and Applications in Psychological Type and Leadership Development* (1997)
Catherine Fitzgerald and Linda K. Kirby (editors)
Davies-Black Publishing
A reference book for professionals in leadership roles who have an understanding of MBTI. Addresses connections between type theory and communication, management of change, decision making and planning and other leadership issues.

*MBTI Applications: A Decade of Research on the Myers-Briggs Type Indicator* (1996)
Allen L. Hammer (Editor)
Consulting Psychologists Press

Summarizes the research conducted on major applications of the MBTI in the last decade. The book contains research on topics such as team-building, management and leadership, health, stress and coping.

*The Type Reporter*
Susan Scanlon, editor
A subscription service of highly readable articles concerning various applications of psychological type. Obtainable from: Susan Scanlon, 11314 Chapel Road, Fairfax Station, VA 22309. Telephone: 703 425 5370. Fax: 703 425 1240.

## Applications in health care

*MBTI Uses in Medicine and other Health Professions 1964–1981*
Isabel Briggs Myers and Mary H. McCaulley
Center for Applications of Psychological Type
Five short papers describing studies of the health professions: the executive summary of monographs 1 and 2, applications of the Myers-Briggs Type Indicator to medicine and other health professions and the Myers longitudinal medical study; the relationship of medical students' psychological type to their specialty twelve years later; the MBTI in medical career planning; relationship of psychological type to drop-out in nursing; prediction of team behavior – how individual differences affect health care teams.

*FLEX Care®*
S.A. Brock and J. Allen (2000)
Brock Associates
A training program for health professionals in the practical use of psychological type for patient and health care team communication.

*Advanced Skills for the Medical Interview using Psychological Type*
G. Plotnicoff and S.A. Brock (in press)
A handbook for physicians which applies psychological type to the patient interview.

# Appendix

## Communication in Healthcare

*Thank you for agreeing to help collect information about what people find important when receiving health care. Each of the questions below gets at a slightly different aspect of what may be important to you. Please answer each question as fully as possible. The information you provide will go for research purposes only.*

I.  First some background:

Check one:   ☐ I work in traditional health care. My job is

_____.

☐ I work in alternative health care (naturopathic, homeopathic, other healing techniques). My job is

_____.

☐ I don't work in health care. My job is

_____.

My current health status:
Check one:

| ☐ none/or few problems | ☐ some problems, <u>not</u> major | ☐ major problem/s |
|---|---|---|

My health status generally in my life:
Check one:

| ☐ none/or few problems | ☐ some problems, <u>not</u> major | ☐ major problem/s |
|---|---|---|

For my health care I use: (Check all that apply)

☐ traditional health care practitioners
☐ alternative health care practitioners
☐ I don't use health care practitioners

My year of birth: 19___    My Myers-Briggs type preference
___ ___ ___ ___ (self-verified)

II. Please answer the following questions . . .
    . . . *if you use* <u>*traditional*</u> *health care practitioners:*

1. When I am consulting with my doctor, what's most important to me is . . . (mention as many items as you'd like)

_____

_____

_____

2. If my doctor delivers bad news to me, I'd like . . . (mention as many items as you'd like)

_____

_____

_____

3. When I receive nursing care – in clinic, in hospital, at home – what's most important to me is . . . (mention as many items you'd like)

_____

_____

_____

4. When I'm helping others receive traditional health care (children, parents, friends, etc.) the most important things I'm looking for from the doctor are:

_____

_____

. . . the most important things I'm looking for from the staff are:

_____

_____

II. Please answer the following questions . . . (continued)
    . . . *if you use <u>alternative</u> health care practitioners:*

   1.  When I receive alternative health care (naturopathic, homeopathic, or other healing techniques), the most important
things I look for are . . . (mention as many items as you'd like)

     _____

     _____

     _____

   2.  If my alternative health care practitioner delivers bad news
to me, I'd like . . . (mention as many items as you'd like)

     _____

     _____

     _____

III. What other comments do you have about what you prefer when
health care professionals communicate with you:

_____

_____

_____

_____

_____

_____

_____

_____

_____

# Bibliography

Allen, J. (1996) "Between the trapezes – making the most of change," *Journal of Nurse Management* 4: 39–43.

Barger, N. and Kirby, L. (1995) *The Challenge of Change in Organizations*, Davies-Black Publishing, Palo Alto, California.

Bayne, R. (1995) *The Myers-Briggs Type Indicator: A Critical Review and Practical Guide*, Chapman and Hall, London.

Bridges, W. (1991) *Managing Transitions – Making the Most of Change*, Addison-Wesley Publishing Company Inc., Reading, Massachusetts.

Bridges, W. (1992) *The Character of Organizations*, Consulting Psychologists Press, Palo Alto, California.

Bridges, W. (1993) *Type your Organization* (Audio-cassette) Infomedix, Garden Grove, California.

Brock S.A. (1987, revised 1992) *The Four-Part Framework*, Center for Applications of Psychological Type, Gainsville, Florida.

Brock, S.A. (1991) *FLEXTalk*, Brock Associates, Minneapolis, Minnesota.

Brock, S.A. (1994) *Using Type in Selling*, Consulting Psychologists Press, Palo Alto, California.

Brock, S.A. (1995) *Type in Practical Influencing: Consulting, Teamwork, Managing, Selling, Living Effectively with Others* (Audio-cassette) Infomedix, Garden Grove, California.

Brock, S.A. (1997) "Strategies for using psychological type to enhance communication," in *Developing Leaders*, ed. C. Fitzgerald and L. Kirby, Davies-Black Publishing, Palo Alto, California.

Brock, S.A. (1999) *FLEXCare*, Brock Associates, Minneapolis, Minnesota.

Buckman, R. (1992) *How to Break Bad News*, Pan, London.

Clark, W.D. (1996) "Doc-patient communication priority at Minn. System," American Academy on Physician and Patient, Woodstock, New York, report in *Modern Healthcare*, December 16th.

Diamond, J. (1999) "John Diamond," *The Times*, London.

Fitzgerald, C. (1997) "Type development and leadership development," in *Developing Leaders: Research and Applications in Psychological Type and Leadership Development*, ed. C. Fitzgerald and L. Kirby, Davies-Black Publishing, Palo Alto, California.

Franks, A. (1997) "Breaking bad news and the challenge of communication," *European Journal of Palliative Care* 4(2): 61–65.

Isachsen, O. and Berens, L. (1988) *Working Together: A Personality Centered Approach to Management*, New World Management Press, Coronado, USA.

Jung, C.G. (1971) *Psychological Types*, Routledge, London.

Kaye, P. (1995) *Breaking Bad News*, EPL Publications, Northampton.

Levinson, W. and Rotter, D. (1993) "The effects of two continuing medical education programs on communication skills of practicing primary care physicians," *Journal of General Internal Medicine* 8: 813–824.

Meichenbaum, D. and Turk, D.C. (1987) *Facilitating Treatment Adherence: A Practitioner's Guidebook*, Plenum, New York.

Myers, I.B., revised by L.K. Kirby and K.D. Myers (1998) *Introduction to Type, Sixth edition*, Consulting Psychologists Press, Palo Alto, California.

Myers, I.B. (1980) *Gifts Differing*, Consulting Psychologists Press, Palo Alto, California.

Myers, I.B. and McCaulley, M. (1985) *Manual: A Guide to the Development and Use of the Myers-Briggs Type Indicator, Second edition*, Consulting Psychologists Press, Palo Alto, California.

Myers, I.B., McCaulley, M.H., Quenk, N.L. and Hammer, A.L. (1998) *Manual: A Guide to the Development and Use of the Myers-Briggs Type Indicator, Third edition*, Consulting Psychologists Press, Palo Alto, California.

Myers, K.D. and Kirby, L.A. (1994) *Type Dynamics and Type Development*, Consulting Psychologists Press, Palo Alto, California.

Pearman, R. and Albritton S. (1997) *I'm Not Crazy, I'm Just Not You*, Davies-Black Publishing, Palo Alto, California.

Quenk, N. (1993) *Beside Ourselves*, Consulting Psychologists Press, Palo Alto, California.

Quenk, N. (1996) *In the Grip*, Consulting Psychologists Press, Palo Alto, California.

Saunders, F.W. (1991) *Katherine and Isabel, Mother's Light, Daughter's Journey*, Consulting Psychologists Press, Palo Alto, California.

Senge, P. (1990) *The Fifth Discipline*, Century Business, Doubleday, New York.

Skynner, R. and Cleese, J. (1983) *Families and How to Survive Them*, Methuen, London.

Spencer, L.M. and Spencer, S.M. (1993) *Competence at Work*, John Wiley and Sons, New York.

# Index

*Index compiled by Frank Pert*